Bigfoot in Pennsylvania

A History of Wild-Men, Gorillas, and Other Hairy Monsters in the Keystone State

compiled, written, and illustrated by

Timothy Renner

BIGFOOT IN PENNSYLVANIA

Copyright © 2017 Timothy Renner

All rights reserved.

CreateSpace Independent Publishing Platform

ISBN: 154551397X
ISBN-13: 978-1545513972

DEDICATION

to Alison, Gideon, and Ursula
who *continue* to endure my fascination with all things strange.

to Catherine and David Diehl.
Thank you for all your help,
a list of which would require a separate volume.

CONTENTS

	Acknowledgments	i
	A Note on Spelling and Grammar - and a Disclaimer	ii
	Introduction	iii
I	The Whistling Wild Boy of the Woods	2
II	Can These Things Be?	7
III	His Eyes Were Very Large and Piercing	16
IV	Monster Gorillas and Unearthly Howls	22
V	Half Man and Half Beast	38
VI	A Black-Bearded Ghoul-Faced Thing	59
VII	An Unknown Monster	103
VIII	Gorilla Attacks	118
	Appendix I: A Nearby Gorilla Report	154
	Appendix II: Mystery Lights	157
	Appendix III: Some Other Strange Creatures in PA	169
	Appendix IV: Alternate Names for Bigfoot in PA	176
	Index of Place Names	179

ACKNOWLEDGMENTS

Edited by Catherine Diehl.

Cover design by Brian Magar.

Some of the names in the appendix *Alternate Names for Bigfoot in Pennsylvania* are from a list of similar worldwide bigfoot names compiled by Colin Schneider aka The Crypto-Kid.

A NOTE ON SPELLING AND GRAMMAR - AND A DISCLAIMER

Regarding "bigfoot" - since this is the name of a group of animals, not one individual, I do not capitalize bigfoot. I also use "bigfoot" as both the singular and plural (like "deer"). Some other authors have tried to standardize the grammar for bigfoot, insisting the plural is variously "bigfeet" or "bigfoots", however to my ears both of these terms hold more problems than simply using the term bigfoot universally as the singular and plural. Until the Oxford English Dictionary weighs in on the subject, I will stand on "bigfoot". Pun intended.

Since the bulk of this volume is taken from old newspaper articles, in most cases I have kept the grammar and spelling as they appeared in the original articles. I believe this retains the flavor of the originals - as does the columned layout. There is something special about reading these old articles. It is very much a window to the past, and I wanted to keep as much of that old view in the window as possible.

Along with the grammar and spelling of the past come the biases and outdated attitudes of long ago. I am, unfortunately for my straining book and record shelves, a bit of a completist. I have made, to the best of my abilities, a complete survey of early "wild-man" articles concerning Pennsylvania. Amongst these reprinted articles you will find some words and attitudes that we no longer consider politically correct - veering, at times, into outright racism. I have included these articles only for their references to what I believe are bigfoot creatures. Reading them today can be an eye-opening experience both in how far we have come as a society and in how many of these hurtful stereotypes have survived amongst modern racists. In no way should the inclusion of said articles be taken as an endorsement or tacit acceptance of the racism, xenophobia, and other backwards beliefs displayed therein. My interest, and hopefully the interest of the reader as well, lies with tales of mysterious creatures, not with the biases and attitudes of racist humans.

INTRODUCTION

Humans have been seeing hairy monsters for as long as we have been keeping records. The Norse people had their trolls; medieval Europe had its wild men; in old England, the wodwose; cave paintings and carvings of the First Nations peoples of the United States and Canada; the list goes on and on. It seems throughout human history, wherever we have lived, hairy wild creatures, massive and upright-walking, have lived in the wilderness just beyond the reach of our lights - be they primitive fires or the most modern LED illuminations.

I have long pondered what this could mean. In his book *Them + Us*, Danny Vendramini makes an interesting argument that modern humans may have been subject to Neanderthal predation. Vendramini extends his theory to explain a host of modern human behaviors and physical traits and asserts that Neanderthal predation may be the single most important factor in making us who we *are*. Vendramini's theories are controversial and not fully accepted by many anthropologists; but even if he is only partially right - even if Neanderthals (or perhaps some other primitive primate relative) only occasionally hunted humans or abducted women - what scars this must have left on our collective psyche!

I once read a theory that the somewhat common experience of feeling like you are falling and jerking awake - usually as you are first fading off to sleep - is some kind of collective sense memory passed down from when humans or proto-humans slept in trees. If this powerful sensation has stayed with us through all of our history, then imagine how much more imbedded would be the images of hairy monsters - bigger; stronger; like us, but unlike us at the same time - monsters who have come to eat us and breed with our women. That would seem as worthy a genetic memory to pass down as any.

This isn't to say I think that bigfoot creatures are just some kind of illusion conjured by our collective unconscious. Illusions don't leave footprints, hair, and scat behind. That said, I don't know *what* these creatures are. I don't think anyone really knows at this point. It has been said, and said truly, that there are no "experts" when it comes to bigfoot.

The bigfoot phenomenon is an incredible puzzle. Every answer will lead to more questions. I don't think you or I or any of the current army of researchers are the ones who get to solve this puzzle. We may participate in the search; we may even get to see the puzzle at a different angle; a lucky few of us may get to lay in a new piece of the puzzle; but we do not get to solve this puzzle. I sincerely hope I am proven wrong about this idea in my lifetime, but I do not think that will be the case.

Many of those same folks who declare that there are no bigfoot experts are also the ones who make sweeping declarations such as 'bigfoot is a physical animal with no special abilities and anyone who puts forth any other theory is foolish'. So much for there being no "experts". Of course, they may be right. However, this seems less and less likely to me the more I dig into the topic.

It is simply true that where you get bigfoot sightings you also get other strange phenomena. Not always, but too often to ignore - around the same places, and around the same time, these *other* things will creep through. Most often this takes the form of mystery lights - be it orbs, will-o-the-wisps, spooklights, or UFOs. It isn't always lights though - you also get ghosts, black dogs, anomalous animals, even other cryptid creatures such as dogmen, goatmen, and the like.

Add to this the number of witnesses who report bigfoot "cloaking" like the creature from the *Predator* movies; others who have witnessed bigfoot creatures disappear or appear from nowhere; yet others who claim the creatures are demonic in nature and abilities.

I find it incredibly ironic that there are groups of people who are fully ready to believe in - and spend time hunting - an 8-foot tall hairy bipedal ape in the American wilderness - yet some of these same people will dismiss reports of this *other* strangeness related to bigfoot as "crazy" or nonsense. As I have said in the past: If you are going to believe one witness saw a giant ape-man in the woods of North America then why are you going to ignore the same witness when he said he saw a UFO at the same time - or a separate witness who reported strange lights down the road from that bigfoot sighting? By doing this, it seems you are missing a potential piece of the puzzle.

In his excellent book, *The Bigfoot Phenomenon in Pennsylvania*, Dr. Paul G. Johnson brings up the idea that bigfoot creatures may have access to some abilities that we do not. Not magical abilities. Not demonic powers. No, Dr. Johnson suggests quantum physics may be the explanation for the bigfoot's seemingly supernatural manifestations. My gut tells me there is something to this - for aspects of quantum physics can seem quite spooky indeed when viewed through the lens of traditional Newtonian physics.

Who can say though? For my part, I believe people are seeing these creatures. Something is leaving footprints, hair, and scat behind. Something is making strange stick formations in the woods. Something is killing and possibly eating pets and livestock. In extreme cases, something is even abducting and killing humans.

This *something* however, seems to understand what cameras are. It avoids even the most perfectly hidden trail cams as if they are flagged with huge blaze orange warning banners. Except for a few pieces of controversial footage, every film or photograph of the creatures seems to be blurry at best. The "blobsquatch" is the most common photographic subject offered by people in this field - followed closely by the pareidolia leaf-face. If it seems like I am making fun, I am not. I think the inability of people to photograph bigfoot clearly is an actual part of the phenomenon. Whether it is the fault of the people; the camera technology; or some distortion manifested by the creatures themselves is yet to be determined.

What this *something* is, is the big question. A physical manifestation of our collective memory? A ghost of a prehistoric hairy hominid? An alien creature dropped here by a flying saucer? A time traveler? A dimensional immigrant? A big ape in the woods? All or none of the above? I don't have the answer at this time. For now, the answer is only that this *something* is bigfoot.

From the reports, it seems there are several different types of bigfoot being witnessed: some are giant and ape-like; some are described as looking more human-like, as if it is a relict hominid of some sort; others are described as ferocious with baboon-like features and clawed hands; and yet others, like the albatwitch or "little people", are described as being no taller than 4-feet, thin and wiry. All of these varieties are covered, more or less, with hair, and all have been reported in Pennsylvania.

Pennsylvania holds a long history of bigfoot sightings. The First Nations tribes knew of the creatures in Pennsylvania before the Europeans ever arrived. The Susquehannock Indians had paintings of the small, hairy albatwitch creatures on their war shields. Tribes to the north told tales of "Stone Giants". The Nanticoke were said to have warned the early European settlers not to follow the lights in the woods - and also to be careful of something which became known in English as The Hidebehind - a creature that would stalk people through the forest, peeking from the trees, often taking the last traveler in line, who would never be seen again. As the Europeans spread across the state, their newspapers started publishing tales of wild-men and strange upright creatures prowling through the forests of Pennsylvania.

As I researched my first book, *Beyond the Seventh Gate*, the single biggest surprise was the sheer number of bigfoot sightings in York, Lancaster, and Adams Counties, Pennsylvania. I had heard of a few of the reports before I started my research and figured I would find a few more, but I was in no way prepared for the quantity of sightings in just three counties.

Quite a few of the sightings in my first book came from old newspaper articles. As the terms "bigfoot" and "sasquatch" were not in common usage until the second half of the 20th century, digging up these old stories requires searching under different terms. Prior to the 1900s, "wild-man" is the most commonly used term for these creatures - though "hairy men", "giants", "hairy giants", and other descriptive names are used at times. Sometimes in Pennsylvania the elusive creatures were called "spooks".

In this volume, I present a statewide survey of historical sightings starting with the earliest reference I could find and ending in the 1920s. Some of these reports are scary; some are matter-of-fact; while others are quite strange. As a collector and investigator of such things, I quite enjoy reading these old accounts. Beyond entertainment, I believe that there is value in these stories to the modern investigator - from the locations and time of year of the sightings to the reported behaviors of the creatures - many of which match up with modern reports of bigfoot behavior.

Reading these "wild-men" articles with a modern eye, it could be tempting to dismiss many of the sightings as "dumb" country-folk misidentifying creatures. Newspapermen prided themselves on being men of reason, and looked for any explanation to dismiss an outrageous story - especially if it was first reported in another paper. As such, at times, we get explanations as varied as a misidentified raccoon(!), wandering itinerants, escaped "lunatics", wild cattle, and, sadly in the light of our racist past, "negroes" sometimes take the blame. In fact, there seems often to be an air of cruel ridicule as the articles dismiss people's observations or exaggerate the physical attributes of a homeless person or an African American.

There are not many country-folk, no matter their level of education, who could confuse a giant hair-covered bipedal creature with a raccoon. I am certain there were misidentifications. I am certain some of the articles herein refer to homeless men, Native Americans, bears, or other wholly natural and common creatures of the woods. Likewise, some articles were no doubt newspaper exaggerations or outright hoaxes. I am also certain there are far too many of these stories for every single one to be a misidentification or hoax.

Many of the newspaper "wild-men" are very tall. Reports of 7 or 8-foot "wild-men" are not uncommon in these stories. Considering men were smaller in the 1800s - the average height being somewhere in the range of 5'5" - it seems unlikely that there was an army of incredibly tall homeless men making their way across the lands. Doubtful too, are the sheer number of "escaped lunatics" which populate these old articles. The walls of those old mental institutions would have had to have looked like Swiss cheese to allow that many escapes.

Most witnesses today, as in the past, are not stupid. Nor are they liars. Hunters can tell the difference between a bear and a bipedal hominid. Farmers know that a cow doesn't walk on two legs. Almost no one on earth could mistake a raccoon for a huge ape-like creature! Likewise, not many people will risk ridicule to make up a tale about a bigfoot creature/wild-man - now or then. The air of superiority taken by some of the writers of these old reports and the derision leveled at the witnesses at times is still echoed today by the boisterous skeptic or the "reasoned" reporter, neither of whom have actually witnessed a single thing themselves. Yet, they are willing to dismiss the experiences of others - and even the expertise of scientists like Dr. Jeff Meldrum who has identified elements of primate anatomy shown in casts of bigfoot footprints which would be impossible for anyone who wasn't a fellow expert to fake.

Many of the articles report these wild-men have long beards and/or long hair but do not mention hair covered bodies as we would expect from bigfoot reports. I believe this is due to the time from which the reports originated. A hair covered humanoid would have been far outside the frame of reference for people of this time. It would be much easier for both witness and reporter to conceive of a man with a beard that hung below his waist or hair that reached the ground, as is often the case in these articles. Many of the wild-man articles do report that the subject was attired in the skin of one animal or another. Alternately, other articles have the wild-men dressed in rags and tatters of clothing. These "rags" could have been body hair, misidentified or mis-reasoned into being tattered cloth. This is mirrored today in sightings wherein witnesses report seeing what they thought at first to be a man in a ghillie suit but which they later realized to be a hair covered hominid.

There may be another factor that accounts for so many of these "wild men" being clothed. The Victorian and Edwardian eras were quite modest, even "puritan" in terms of what was considered acceptable in society. It could be that naked wild men and women were considered just too risque to feature in print. Perhaps, either reporters or editors "clothed" them so as not to upset the modest minds of their readers.

This isn't to say there couldn't have been misidentifications and outright hoaxes. These occurred in the past as well as today, and certainly some of the reports herein could be based on misidentification or hoaxes. However, newspaper articles often noted these misidentifications as well. I read and discarded many many articles wherein someone was first thought a "wild-man" but was later identified as a common human by name, language, or action. In some cases, these "wild-men" do seem to be humans with mental illness of some sort. Many wild-man articles end with someone being taken to the county home. For every wild-man article that *could* be about a bigfoot creature, there are probably ten or twenty which are decisively about humans. These articles are not printed in this volume as they add little to the discussion at hand. It is likely that many of the articles I have included *do* refer to humans. Unless the person was caught or held a conversation with someone, it is impossible to know for sure. If there were feral people in Pennsylvania - wholly human, but fully wild - I think this too should be of interest to both the average reader and bigfoot enthusiast. As to the articles that *do* appear in this volume: I leave it up to the reader to decide how many are possible bigfoot creatures or other strange entities, how many are hoaxes, and how many are simply humans.

In 1869 Mark Twain "interviewed" a wild-man for newspapers. It was a parody, of course; a send-up of these wild-man articles appearing in the papers of the time. Interestingly, Twain's fictional wild-man claimed to be the son of the biblical Cain. Cain's offspring have often been noted as "monsters" - *Beowolf*'s Grendel perhaps most famously. Even today, many researchers have tried to make connections between bigfoot creatures and the Nephilim from the Bible, a race of giants who were said to be the offspring of fallen angels and human females.

Notice as the newspaper articles move closer to the 1900s, some witnesses begin to describe "gorillas" instead of wild-men. As circuses and carnivals made their way through both cities and small-town

America, and as newspapers began to publish photographs of exotic creatures "discovered" abroad (the mountain gorilla being one of them), more and more people became exposed to our simian brethren. They now had a reference other than a wild human. We begin to see terms like "gorilla", "ape-man", "monkey-man", and the like pop up, eventually replacing the "wild-man" as more common descriptors. That is, until the terms bigfoot and sasquatch become common currency, starting sometime in the 1950s and continuing through today.

Notice, too, how the newspaper explanations shift from "escaped lunatics" to gorillas escaping from zoos, circuses, or menageries. Gorillas were an extremely expensive exotic animal - a live specimen could fetch as much as $20,000.00 at the time - which is, conservatively, the equivalent of about $500,000.00 in today's money. Not many live gorillas were even in the U.S. at the time - simply because most circuses and zoos couldn't afford them. The captive gorillas that were here were all named and rather famous (their activities being often reported in the papers of the day). There simply wasn't a surplus of gorillas to escape and wander through the hills of Pennsylvania.

In the following pages we walk through history, and through Penn's Woods, with hairy creatures pacing us and fiery eyed giants peeking from the trees. Mad ape-men scream and wave their arms as if to say "we have always been here and we will always be, no matter what name you place upon us." Let's follow their footprints and see where they lead.

I. THE WHISTLING WILD BOY OF THE WOODS

1838 - 1847

STRANGE ANIMAL, OR FOOD FOR THE MARVELOUS.

— Something like a year ago, there was considerable talk about a strange animal, said to have been seen in the south-western part of Bridgewater. Although the individual who described the animal persisted in declaring that he had seen it, the story was heard and looked upon, more as food for the marvelous, than as having any foundation in fact. He represented the animal, as we have it through a third person, as having the appearance of a child seven or eight years old, though somewhat slimmer, and covered entirely with hair. He saw it, while picking berries, walking toward him erect, and whistling like a person. After recovering from the fright, he is said to have pursued it, but it ran off with such speed, whistling as it went, that he could not catch it. He said it ran like the "devil," and continued to call it after that name.

The same, or a similar looking animal, was seen in Silver Lake township, about two weeks since, by a boy of some sixteen years old. We had the story from the father of the boy, in his absence, and afterwards from the boy himself. The boy was sent to work in the back woods, near the New York state line — He took with him a gun, and was told by his father to shoot anything he might see, except persons or cattle. After working a while, he heard some person, a little brother as he supposed, coming towards him, whistling quite merrily. It came within a few rods of him and stopped. He said it looked like a human being, covered with black hair, about the size of his brother, who was six or seven years old. His gun was some little distance off, and he was very much frightened. He, however, got his gun, and shot at the animal, but trembled so that he could not hold still. The strange animal, just as his gun "went off," stepped behind a tree, and then ran off whistling as before. The father said the boy came home very much frightened, when thinking about the animal he had seen, he would to use his own words, "burst out a crying."

Making due allowance for frights and consequent exaggeration, an animal of singular appearance has doubtless been seen. What it is, or whence it came, is of course yet a mystery. From the description, if an ourang outang were known to be in this country, we might think this to be it. As no such animal is known, (without vouching for the correctness of the story,) we shall leave the reader to conjecture, or guess for himself, what it is. For the sake of a name, however, we will call the "strange animal" The Whistling Wild Boy of the Woods. Why is not this story as good as that copied into the Volunteer of week before last, relative to the wild boy of Indiana? We acknowledge that the story has excited somewhat our propensity for the marvelous, and we give it, as much as any thing, to gratify the same propensity in others.[1]

---◆---

☛There is a story among our country folks that there is a *wild man in the woods* in the neighborhood of Easton, and females are actually afraid to come to town alone. We know of several *wild men* in the Borough — and there are no doubt some in the country. — Argus.[2]

---◆---

A STRANGE STORY, and whether true or not, our readers can best judge after they have read it.

What Is It? — A strange being lately made its appearance in the vicinity of our Exchange, which has been the cause of much wonder, and a good deal of alarm, when seen by females and the more timorous of the other sex. Children intuitively clung more closely to their mothers, and all were observed to step lighter and quicker when near it. Numerous and various have been the conjectures what this ominous being was, and where it came from; but none cared to satisfy their curiosity by too close an approximation to the object of their astonishment. It was about five feet high, stood erect, and its features completely enveloped in long hair, as black and glossy as the raven's plume. Some said it was Robinson Crusoe, clothed in his goat skin habits; but this was improbable, for the last account we have of that renowned hero states that he was then near four score years old, while this nondescript was evidently much younger. Others said it was probably Orson, the wild man of the woods, or the wild child lately seen about a certain lake in Michigan; and again, others said it was the Chimpanzee which had escaped from its keepers; but it could not be either of these, for we have an undoubted recount of the death of the former, and it was evidently too large for either of the latter. It could not be a large Newfoundland dog, nor a bear, for dogs always run on four legs, and bears do not always go on two.

What is it? was the constant inquiry, and the mystery is now solved by the courage of two loafers who were feeling in their tenantless pockets for what had long ceased to abide there, and ruminating on the prospects of a bed in the watch-house or gutter, without a supper, and of a dry and thirsty morning, fell in with the hero of our tale near the Girard Bank.

"Necessity is the mother of invention," and accordingly they determined upon its immediate capture, for exhibition to wondering and gaping crowds. Fortune now ceased to frown, and golden dreams of wealth and splendor were before them. No longer would they trudge foot in the dirty streets. No longer go supperless to bed — nor that bed be the bottom of a watch-box. No longer rise in the morning with killing thirst and nothing to allay it. No — perish the thought — "Richard's himself again." Fearing nought but the escape of this anomalous being, upon which their hopes depended, they instantly seized it, and all their dreams of glory vanished like the morning cloud or the fleeting visions of a midnight hour, and left them in disappointment and despair — for it proved to be a poor fellow who had been so unfortunate as to tumble head foremost into a can of Dr. Jayne's Hair Tonic, and who now remained a monument — proof positive — of the extraordinary virtues of the article.[3]

[1] *The Baltimore Sun* (Baltimore, MD), August 3, 1838.

Here we have two accounts of smaller, hair covered bipedal creatures. The fact that they are of slight build and whistling would seem to indicate they are albatwitch type creatures, not just small or young bigfoot. Some legends local to Columbia, PA (where the albatwitch are said to make their home, near Chickie's Rock) state that the creatures communicate to each other by whistling. Some people even claim to have mastered a complex whistling pattern, heard in the woods around Columbia, which acts as a sort of "welcome" call between albatwitch and can, if whistled correctly, draw the creatures out of hiding. For more information on albatwitch, see my previous book, *Beyond the Seventh Gate*.

[2] *The Wilkes-Barre Advocate* (Wilkes-Barre, PA), October 16, 1839.

[3] *Public Ledger* (Philadelphia, PA), January 30, 1847.

This story takes quite a turn and we are left to guess if it is in part or whole an attempt at humor, a desperate grasp at explaining away the hairy creature, or some kind of advertisement for Dr. Jayne's Hair Tonic. The first part of the article seems to be standard reporting and my guess is that the latter part of the article, regarding the two "loafers", was reporter invention - the purpose of which is lost to time.

II. CAN THESE THINGS BE ?

1859 - 1875

WILD PEOPLE. — In Lancaster, Pa., a thing like a man, but hairy as a bear, has been seen frequently by the people. It is very wild and strong. It was once seen in a cow pen, sucking the cows, and when discovered it started as if about to fight, then turned and fled, bounding like a deer. It walks upright, and is supposed to be a wild man.[1]

———◆———

A WILD MAN has been discovered in a forest in Clearfield county. He was covered all over with a copper-colored down, and when captured was able to speak only one word — "craft." He had forgotten all the rest of the English language. Ex-Governor Bigler took the wild man in his hands, and will prepare him to vote for the Democratic candidate in October. This story may be true, since large numbers of the residents fled to the woods during the late draft. Many are yet missing, so that more wild men may yet be caught.[2]

———◆———

Blair county has a "wild man of the woods."[3]

———◆———

A WILD WOMAN. — Gebhartsville, Somerset county, Pa. claims the sensation of the week. It has a genuine, simon-pure, wild woman, almost as nude as was Eve after the fall, for she wears only an apron of leaves, sandals of bark, and a necklace of tea-berries. Swift as a doe, people have rarely been able to see her features distinctly in her visits to the neighboring farm houses and outskirts of the village; yet those who have seen her declare that she is far from uncomely in person and countenance. Her oval face is set with keen black eyes, and framed in long masses of flowing black hair; and with her tall, slender figure, she has the air of the Queen of the forests. Like most women, she has a great dread of men, and bounds away over fences and fields whenever one attempts to approach her. Yet she is consistent, and avoids in like manner too great familiarity with women.

For children, however, she seems to have great fondness, as was exemplified only a few days past. While passing near the house of a farmer she espied a little girl three or four years old playing in the road. Crouching, she crawled behind a fence until within a short distance of the child, then, with a bound, cleared the fence, in the next moment seized the screaming little one, and was away at the top of her speed. The mother, hearing the screams of her child, pursued, screaming yet more loudly. Her husband, attracted by the cries of both, hastened to the chase. The wild woman, finding herself encumbered by the weight of the child, dropped it and escaped. The latter was uninjured, with the exception of some scratches, which, no doubt, are attributable to the long nails of the strange denizen of the fields and forest.[4]

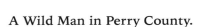

A Wild Man in Perry County.

Considerable excitement prevails among the different parties frequenting the mountains in search of berries five miles west of Harrisburg and directly opposite Rockville. Not long since John Quincy Adams of the latter place while at his leisure was in pursuit of berries and having wandered a considerable distance into the mountains became terribly alarmed at the appearance of a man supposed to be perfectly wild, and going about in a condition that according to description, would be sufficient to put to flight the boldest backwoodsman. At least the sight of the human monster was too much for "Quincy" who vacated the grounds with the speed of a flying buffalo. He never venturing to cast a look behind but leaping the smaller bushes, dodging overhanging tree, losing his hat, and relieving himself of his bucket he very rapidly increased the distance twixt him and his starting point, with the dreaded terror a considerable way in the rear a bellowing out his wild yells of triumph, but losing ground in the pursuit. By the remarkably rapid strides of the venerable "Quincy" (not the Quincy that formerly sat on the Presidential stool however) he soon found himself in sight of the cozy little village where in an elderly lady's mansion he might find relief, and as was necessary a camphor stimulant. He has not been to gather berries since, and no further developments of the mystery have been gained, save that two of the Telegraph operations, (of which there are four employed in the place by the different R.R. Co's) saw fit one day since to rusticate among the shady trees and "dispatch" any whortleberries that might fall in their way, and finding themselves a smart distance outside the bounds of safety and hearing the "calls" of their instruments when they were startled suddenly by some unusual noise, and after reconnoitering some little with a view to finding out the why and wherefore (in which they failed,) they convened and held a council of war and concluded to quit the place.[5]

———— ◆ ————

— Ruchsville is in Carbon County, we believe. A naked wild man has been "making afraid" the neighborhood for some time without affording a clue to his particular habitation. Grant or Greeley must be responsible for the freaks of this nondescript.[6]

———— ◆ ————

The latest rumor is that our quiet town is the abode of a "wild man," who wanders about in the darkness of night, entirely naked. We understand that several parties declare they have seen him. One of these, being interviewed, declared he never saw the strange individual, never said he saw him, and never before heard of him. Wonder if it might not be the Carlisle "ghost" or tramp?[7]

———— ◆ ————

It is reported that a "spook" made its appearance, in the shape of a wild man, in Bottstown, on Friday night last. He has created quite an excitement among some of the more superstitious citizens of that place.[8]

---♦---

A prevailing superstition amongst the Dutch is that of the "hairy man," the wild man of the mountains, a being without other clothing than hirsute abundance, who climbs lofty trees, afflicts children and stock, and defies pursuit and capture. Only last week this ancient adventurer was reported in the Reading papers as having been seen on Welsh Mountain, and the sagacious editor added: "It is high time that this formidable monster was brought to terms and put under durance."[9]

---♦---

HAMBURG, July 22, 1873.

A wild man is said to have been seen on the Blue Mountain, in Upper Bern township, last week, by a man who drove his cattle on the mountain. He says that the man is in nude condition, and that his entire body is covered with hair about three inches in length. After the man had driven his cattle to the desired place he went home and got some neighbors to go along up the mountain to catch the "critter," but he had disappeared, and their search was unsuccessful. Some think that the whole thing is a hoax, while others think otherwise.[10]

---♦---

A WILD MAN. — A sensation of a new order is now exciting the people of Hanover, York county. A wild man has been seen in Saeger's woods, on several occasions, by individuals who are willing to take an oath to the fact. He is described as being attired in woman's clothes, face masked, and a large black dog following at his heels. The neighborhood is greatly excited at the appearance of the strange looking object, and the young men are about forming themselves into a band for the purpose of capturing him.[11]

---♦---

The Wild Man, the Wild Beast and the Big Snake.

Every year about this time Morgantown, situated on the confines of Lancaster, Berks and Chester counties, becomes excited over a wild man of immense stature and terrible aspect, who haunts the mountains in the vicinity of that village. Later in the season they are annually troubled with a wild beast, of unknown species, which strikes terror into the hearts of the inhabitants. During the summer the scourge of the neighborhood is a huge serpent, varying in length from 15 to 10 feet, and whose chief delight seems to be to frighten women and children away from the blackberry and huckleberry patches for which that vicinity is noted. The snake story is a very good one, and serves a very good purpose in keeping timid people out of the woods, and thus permitting the professional berry gatherers to reap the harvest unmolested by juvenile competition; but for the life of us we cannot see the expediency of starting out the wild man every fall and the wild beast every winter. What good purpose can they possibly serve the Morgantowners that they are thus remorselessly compelled to walk along the "ragged edge" of the ridge all the way from Adamstown to Parkesburg? And yet the wild man has been already trotted out. He is, according to the statements of those who have seen him, nearly seven feet high, and weighs over two hundred and fifty pounds; he walks generally on all fours, is almost covered with hair, gives unearthly yells and makes all kinds of gestures. His hands and feet are double the size of an ordinary man's and he presents an altogether horrible appearance. He approaches the cabins of settlers in the mountains, carries off their pigs and sheep, and with a demoniac laugh disappears in the dense forests. The brave spirits of the neighborhood go gunning for him, but whenever they come in sight the monster just gives a yell and a jump, and before the hunters have time to pull trigger he is gone.

Now of what use to the Morgantowners is this wild man? They certainly do not trot him out for nothing. They must have an object in view, but what it is we are at a loss to determine. Won't somebody enlighten us as to the use of this monster as also to the use of their wild beast of unknown species, which haunts the forest every winter?

Since the above was written intelligence reaches us that the beast is already on its travels. It has put in an appearance near Parkesburg; has been seen by several persons none of whom can describe its appearance or the unearthly tones of its voice. It is simply terrible and of ferocious aspect. We wait with much interest its appearance at Morgantown.[12]

———————◆———————

— The Berks county wild man, who haunts the mountain in the neighborhood of Swatara Gap, has been seen again. He is said to be over seven feet high, with a face and body covered with hair, walks on his hands and feet like a beast, and jumps ten feet at a time with apparent ease.[13]

―――――◆―――――

Some of your readers in speaking of the "wild man," and other things of which I have written, ask "can these things be?" I reply, "They be."[14]

―――――◆―――――

[1] *The Plumas Argus* (Quincy, CA), March 3, 1859.

[2] *The Pittsburgh Gazette* (Pittsburgh, PA), September 16, 1865.
An odd little story - the man being covered in "copper-colored down" certainly makes me think of bigfoot creatures - but the fact that he - or it - was captured would seem to indicate that this was probably just a man. I am more swayed to the idea that this was a human and not a creature by its capture than I am by it speaking. There have been multiple witness accounts of bigfoot creatures speaking - both in their own language and various human languages. This may be nothing more than mimicry on the part of the bigfoot, but no one can say for certain.

[3] *Huntingdon Journal*, (Huntingdon, PA) June 6, 1871.

[4] *Harrisburg Telegraph*, (Harrisburg, PA) November 18, 1871.
A somewhat rarer "wild woman" story. Besides her strange dress, note how easily she leaps over fences. This is mentioned twice in the article. The last paragraph is rather disturbing as there are many modern reports of bigfoot creatures taking special interest in human children as well as First Nations legends stating that the creatures would sometimes abduct women and children.

[5] *The New Bloomfield Times* (New Bloomfield, PA), August 13, 1872.

[6] *Pittston Gazette* (Pittston, PA), October 10, 1872.

[7] *The York Daily* (York, PA), November 4, 1872.

[8] *The York Daily* (York, PA), December 10, 1872.

[9] *Reading Times* (Reading, PA), January 6, 1873.

[10] *Reading Times* (Reading, PA), July 23, 1873.

[11] *The York Daily* (York, PA), August 11, 1874.
One of the stranger wild men we will meet in this volume. While this article almost certainly refers to a human "wild man" it is interesting that he is followed by a large black dog - black dogs figuring prominently into many Pennsylvania legends and hauntings. It is also interesting that this wild man is reported as having his face masked. One wonders what the mask looked like - was it a simple veil of some sort, or the visage of a monster?

[12] *Reading Times* (Reading, PA), September 22, 1874.

On the other hand, this "wild man" is almost certainly a bigfoot. Many behaviors noted in this article are still reported by bigfoot witnesses today.

First, the height of the creature is noted at almost seven feet, with hands and feet twice the size of an ordinary man. The "unearthly" howls, carrying off of livestock, and leaping away from pursuers are all often noted in bigfoot reports.

The creature's means of locomotion - walking on all fours - may give some pause: After all, bigfoot is supposed to be bipedal, right? Actually, a surprising number of reports, both modern and antiquated, tell of the creatures switching easily from bipedal walking or running to moving across the ground on hands and feet.

The mention of giant snakes is something which seems to appear in a few of these old "wild-man" articles - not just in Pennsylvania but from abroad as well. This is something which does not seem to have carried over into modern bigfoot reports, but it is nevertheless an interesting feature I found worthy of note.

[13] *The Pittsburgh Daily Commercial* (Pittsburgh, PA), September 24, 1874.

[14] *Daily Record of the Times* (Wilkes-Barre, PA), February 2, 1875.

III. HIS EYES WERE VERY LARGE AND PIERCING

1876 - 1877

— The *Mercer Dispatch* revives the wild man sensation. It locates him in Madison township, Clarion county. The article is too diaphanous.[1]

A wild man is the latest sensation at Bennington, Blair county. The nondescript is fat and hairy, with a red face, and amuses himself by throwing stones at barns and chasing females.[2]

Blair county's latest sensation is a "wild man," who is said to have been seen twice in the neighborhood of Bennington Furnace.[3]

THAT "WILD MAN"

Hughesville and the Surrounding Country Greatly Excited - A Hunting Party on His Trail.

Hughesville and vicinity have been in a state of excitement for a few days past, on account of the rumor that a wild man has been seen in the woods near that place. The report was not fully credited until a few days ago, when the strange object was seen by Hon. George Steck and others, in a corn field owned by Mr. Steck. The news spread like wildfire and the excitement was terrible. Every able-bodied man ran for his gun, and a company of thirty or forty men and boys, fully armed, was immediately formed, and started in pursuit of the object, resolved to solve the mystery. It is reported to be a very large man, entirely naked and very shy, running swiftly away when approached by any one. The searching party returned late the same day, not having been successful in capturing the mysterious being, although several of the party claim to have seen it — at some distance. It is probably some lunatic, who, to suit his mad fancy, has taken to the woods, there to end his wretched days. Another party to start out immediately to see what they can do.[4]

———◆———

A few weeks since, Wilber Ramey, aged twelve years, in company with others, was on the Allegheny mountain for berries. The party becoming thirsty dispatched young Ramey for a pail of water, the nearest known spring being about half a mile distant along the old Watson road. After arriving at the spring he placed his vessel under the spout extending from the spring and sat down to remain until it was full. Scarcely had he seated himself until he saw before him approaching the spring, and apparently coming from a dense ravine, a frightful spectacle. It was the form of a nude human being, except that the form was covered with hair. The hair on the head and face was very long and dark in color. The hair on the body and limbs being much shorter. The hearts of his hands and soles of his feet were the only parts not covered with hair. His eyes were very large and piercing and his arms unusually long. He came to the spring with two small wooden spouts, and after placing an end of one into an end of the other he drank by means of these spouts, continually eyeing young Ramey without uttering a word. Ramey through excitement remarked that "there were men up along the road waiting till he would get them a drink." This caused the unwelcome stranger to glance up the road, the only time his eyes released the boy, who got his bucket and started to retrace his steps up the mountain side when the man disappeared in the bushes. Young Ramey was so badly frightened that for several hours afterward he ate nothing, and in his sleep for several nights succeeding he would become excited and speak of the "wild man." Rumors have it that tracks of bare feet have since been seen in several places on the mountain.[5]

A wild woman, half naked, very dirty, brown colored, roams the woods between Sam City and Slam Bang. She is doubtless a deranged gypsy.[6]

A Wild Man.

Newfield has come to the front with a hairy wild man, so awful mysterious and formidable that he opens up a new field for thought and investigation. He has been seen by some of the most unimpeachable residents of, and visitors to, South Section. He is described as over six feet tall, clad in rough and scanty attire, and wearing a grizzly beard that reaches almost to his knees. Although he has chased several fishermen who have invaded his secluded domain in quest of brook trout, and shot a peaceable farmer near Newfield station, no active steps have been made toward his capture, and he yet roams at large. His latest and most daring exploit occurred about a week ago, when he left the gloom of the forest and actually entered an unoccupied dwelling in the broad light of day. Large and heavy as the wild man is, he glides so swiftly and silently that he frequently is at hand before his coming has been observed. In this silent, ghost-like manner he is said to have floated into the house of a farmer named Payne. The farmer and three companions were engaged in an interesting game of euchre and were not aware of the wild man's company. Payne felt something bushy touching the back part of his head, when, looking up, he found it to be the great beard of the strange hermit. Payne jumped to his feet, and would have struck the silent visitor with a chair, but he avoided the blow, and with mysterious steps made his way to an adjoining room and stretched himself upon a bed. Payne followed him and again raised the chair to strike him, but again he seemed to glide from beneath it, and this time he made his exit through the window by a gliding snake-like motion, but as silently as a wreath of smoke ascends to the blue ether. The farmer watched him and saw him leave his premises and enter a patch of woods near by, and supposed he had disappeared for good, but during the evening of that same day he returned and was seen standing under a tree near the house as though deliberating whether to enter the house. After standing there a short time he turned around suddenly and ran rapidly back to the woods. Next day one of the farmer's cows strayed away and he started off to look for it. Shortly after he left the house, his family heard the sharp crack of a rifle, and in a few minutes back came Payne, pale and breathless, and well-nigh done for. As soon as he could set the machinery of speech in motion he described in graphic language the cause of his excitement. It was an encounter with the wild man. He said he was walking through a clearing calling "ko boss, ko boss," when without warning he heard a rifle discharged close by and felt the wind of a bullet as it whistled over his forehead through the rim of his felt hat and through his erect hair. He fell flat upon the ground, partially stunned, and it was well he did, for the wild man, thinking his first shot had proved fatal, shouldered his piece and strode off into the underbrush. This strange episode is at present the theme of uppermost all through South Section, and it is said that a posse of hunters are preparing to track the wild man, and if possible effect his capture alive or dead.[7]

———————◆———————

[1] *Titusville Herald* (Titusville, PA), August 21, 1876.

[2] *Harrisburg Daily Independent* (Harrisburg, PA), January 20, 1877.
Many of the wild man accounts are but brief articles. This one is of particular interest as it notes stone-throwing, an oft-documented bigfoot behavior.

[3] *Huntingdon Journal* (Huntingdon, PA), January 26, 1877.
Bennington is now a ghost town, but it is of interest that this creature was seen near the Bennington Furnace. I have documented many instances of paranormal activity (including bigfoot and other cryptids) at multiple old furnace sites in Pennsylvania.

[4] *Williamsport Sun-Gazette* (Williamsport, PA), August 4, 1877.

[5] *Altoona Evening Mirror* (Altoona, PA), October 6, 1877.

[6] *Bradford Daily Era* (Bradford, PA), July 24, 1879.

[7] *The Indiana Progress* (Indiana, PA), September 18, 1879.
Many of the features of this wild man report seem to point to something with superhuman capabilities: the silence of his approach, the gliding ghost-like movements, the inability of his pursuers to capture him - or even lay a hand on him. It is only the end of the story wherein the wild man shoots a rifle at farmer Payne that the tale seems to indicate this wild man was human. It remains an interesting report, however, with enough strangeness that I felt it warranted inclusion in this collection.

IV. MONSTER GORILLAS AND UNEARTHLY HOWLS

1881 - 1889

— A Monster gorilla is reported to have made its appearance on Jimmy Brunt's farm, Valley township, Armstrong county. The other night the animal visited the house of John Emory and captured a dog, which he carried away into the woods. Subsequently, it is said, the animal attacked and badly wounded a gigantic hound belonging to Mr. Con. Nulton. A party is organizing to effect his capture.[1]

———————◆———————

A Welsh Mountain Story.

A gentleman living near Morgantown, Berks county, was in town the other day, and tells another "Wild Man of the Woods" story about New California hills, a portion of the Welsh Mountain range. He says a party of young gentlemen were out sleighing with their ladies, and while driving through a pass in the hills the foremost horse suddenly became unmanageable and evinced all the signs of great terror. At the same time a wild cry came from the thicket, causing the horse to turn around, and all efforts to make him pass the place were unavailing. The young men remained near the hills for some minutes, and heard the noise a number of times. The same gentleman says that the farmers in the vicinity have suffered from the depredations of some animal, which makes peculiar footprints in the snow, but up to this time have not been able to discover it, though the hills have been scoured a number of times. Some think the animal is a catamount or an animal of its species. Whether there is anything in the story or not we do not know, but we give it for what it is worth.[2]

———◆———

A wild man has been seen by hunters on Brush Mountain, not far from Altoona.[3]

———◆———

While some Altoona sportsmen were out gunning on Brush Mountain, a few days ago, they discovered a wild man. They say he had long hair and a haggard looking face.[4]

———◆———

A Spook.

— For several weeks past quite a sensation has been created among the residents of Abbottstown street by the nightly appearance on that thoroughfare of a 'Spook,' who is described by those who have chanced to catch a glimpse of it, as a hideous looking affair, assuming respectively the form of a man and that of a bear. The ghostly visitant appears between the hours of 11 and 12 o'clock — about the time of night when certain young gallants say 'Bye, bye,' upon leaving the residence of their lady loves situate in that part of town, and the fact of its presence has caused a number of timid young gentlemen to diminish the number of their visits and hasten the hour of departure. Several parties have been chased at a late hour by the 'Spook,' to whom it has appeared in its dual form of a man and a bear, and they describe it as being a most terrifying object. The excitement continues unabated in that section of the town in regard to the 'Spook,' and the more timid refrain from being out on the street later than 10 o'clock.[5]

———◆———

A Wild Woman of the Mountains.

SHENANDOAH, July 6. — The people of this place are commenting over information received this afternoon that a wild woman, in a semi-nude condition, is roaming around on the Ringtown Mountain, several miles distant. She was seen by a number of boys who were spending the day on the mountains. She was eating something which the boys think was a dead chicken, and continued her meal heedless of them until they came within a few yards, when she jumped up and started after them. She chased them for a short distance, then turned in another direction and disappeared. It is believed that the unfortunate woman is one of the lunatics who escaped from the Dauphin County Almshouse during the fire. The authorities will make an effort to capture her.[6]

———————◆———————

THE WILD WOMAN

Later Developments in the Mystery of Ringtown Woods.

Later developments lead to the belief that the wild woman in the Ringtown woods, near Shenandoah, who chased several lads a few days ago, is the missing Mrs. Gensler, of St. Clair. Her friends scoured the woods in search of her, but failed to capture her. It is believed that she has taken refuge in some of the mine caverns between here and Ringtown. A strict watch will be kept at all times for her reappearance. Mrs. Gensler, about three weeks ago, took several children walking in a wood. She disappeared at the time, leaving the children in the thicket, and has not been heard of since — unless the wild woman is she. She was, apparently, perfectly sane when she started out with the children.[7]

———————◆———————

— The periodical stories of wild men and sea serpents have ceased to excite much interest, and now an Austinburgh correspondent tells of a veritable wild man, or a man reported to be wild, right at home. He is clothed in rags, with scarcely enough of them to cover his body, and both hair and whiskers reaching below his waist. He has been seen but a few times.[8]

───◆───

An alleged wild man is said to be prowling around the upper end of Ligonier Valley.[9]

───◆───

"At Petrolia the people were out looking for a wild man. They hadn't lost one, but they seemed anxious to find this one, because he was chiefly engaged in butchering sheep and things that are usually left around loose in the fields out there. Before the wild man came to disturb them a long-headed old citizen had been robbed for a third time by masked burglars. He had the habit of keeping a hundred thousand dollars or so stuck away in coffee pots, stockings, old boots, and such, because he didn't believe in banks. The folks were so broke up over the wild man that I thought it would be too bad to mention business to them, so I grabbed my gripsack and shook the place."

These, and a dozen other similar items, are an indirect reflection on the quality of the liquor now sold in Western Pennsylvania.[10]

───◆───

The mysterious wild man that caused much excitement in this locality last fall is again frequenting his old haunts and has been seen by a number of our citizens during the past week.[11]

───◆───

The "Wild Man" is still seen occasionally along the creek near Forks. Where he came from, what he eats, where he sleeps, who he is, where he will go, and what he is there for, are all mysteries yet to be solved.[12]

───◆───

— Bridgeville has a wild man. He is of gigantic size and was almost naked when taken. He is thought to have escaped from Washington county.[13]

───◆───

Our quiet neighborhood was disturbed a few evenings ago by what was supposed to be a wild man. He generally kept to the woods and buckwheat fields. He was pursued by five men and a dog (in imagination), but out-winded them all.[14]

— Jackson claims to have a horrid-looking wild man, seven and a half feet high, hairy, and a frequenter of the lakes near the Capitol.[15]

We received a telephone message from Luzerne borough yesterday, stating that there was great excitement there. "A wild man has been found, almost killed by a Coon." Such is life.[16]

A WILD WOMAN FOUND.

A Mystery That Has Disturbed a Neighborhood Made Clear.

Womelsdorf, December 29. For several months the citizens of this village (situated near the foot of the South Mountain, a range of the Alleghenies) have been disturbed by the most unearthly yells coming from the hills. It was generally supposed that they emanated from some strange animal, which had taken refuge in the rocks. Mr. Griesemer, of the Bethany Orphans Home, a Reformed Church institution at the foot of the mountain, several times heard the screams. Franklin Katterman, Jacob Matthews, and Theodore Startze, all old hunters, followed up a trail for several hours, but were finally obliged to give up, as they were led far up into the mountain fastness. Stones and huge rocks were rolled down the hill in their path, and they were obliged to dodge the missiles every now and then.

Theodore Startze says he saw a living thing, half human, half beast. He stood still, the blood chilling in his veins. He had his gun with him, but he dared not shoot. He next started on a run, and to use his own words flew down the hill and did not stop until he got home, not taking time to look whether the beast was following him or not. A party of employees at the Robesonia furnace shot at the beast, but missed it. It is reliably stated that the managers of the furnace offered $200 for the animal alive and $100 for its dead body. For some weeks every person has given the mountain a wide berth. Several farmers also lost sheep and chickens.

Today the mystery was cleared up. A party of Womelsdorf hunters scoured the mountain. They found human footsteps in the snow, which they tracked to a rude hut — a charcoal-burner's deserted cabin. Here they found a young woman, probably twenty-five years of age. She was thinly dressed, her surroundings were uncouth and she appeared much frightened. She has a wild and haggard look and who she is no one knows. She will probably be removed to the Poorhouse. She threw stones down the mountain and yelled to scare the people away. She is of muscular build and many think she has been following this kind of life for years, judging by her general appearance. She has shown the strength of an Amazon and the people have decided to let her alone until the authorities take her in charge.[17]

◆

WHERE IS THE "WILD MAN?"

A Character Who Afforded Blood-Curdling Food for Reading Correspondents.

The doings, adventures, and desperate deeds of Abe Buzzard. the Lancaster county outlaw — or rather *hero* — and the interview that he has been holding with that famous robber, have caused a certain Reading newspaperman to lose sight of an old acquaintance, who must still be alive though neglected by his journalistic friend. We allude to the "Wild Man of the Welsh Mountain," who was so terrifically written up several years ago in the paper with which the aforesaid reporter was and is still connected. We remember the thrilling and eminently truthful descriptions of the "Wild Man," who was portrayed as rushing over the rocks and ravines of the mountains on all fours, his eyes glaring wildly, fire blazing from his nostrils, and his mouth foaming with gore and fury — altogether a being of horrible shape and aspect. This fierce looking object was seen by several persons, as
"O'er the rough and rugged rocks
   the ragged rascal ran."—
And even the Reading reporter caught sight of him once or twice

— from the back window of his office. And this about the season of the year when the "Wild Man" generally makes his debut on the Welsh mountains, and no doubt he is there now, all the same — if Abe Buzzard has not slain him — and just as open to interviews as he was a few years ago. We submit that it was a shame to neglect such a fellow, and that no stories about infants seen swinging in cradles in the tops of trees; no desperate adventure of hunters with lynxes, wild cats, or contests between Hungarian wood choppers and bears of enormous size, in northern Berks; no fearful ghost scenes witnessed by belated travelers away up toward Hamburg; no battles on the South mountain between huge snakes, which finally swallow each other; no startling stories of Abe Buzzard taking part in prayer meetings; nor yet the recent bringing out of the wild woman of Womelsdorf, will compensate the reading public of the state of Berks county, and "the rest of mankind," for the loss of the "Wild Man of the Welsh Mountains." The Reading man who has the copyright and patent to this truly wonderful personage, will please tell us all he knows about him, and his welfare and history for the past few years.[18]

_____◆_____

A Wild Man in the Mountains.

A wild man is reported on the Lehigh Mountain, near Allentown. He leaves his hiding place between 9 and 10 o'clock nightly and keeps up an unearthly howling nearly all night. He is supposed to be an escaped lunatic.[19]

_____◆_____

A Wild Man on the Lehigh Mountain.

Considerable excitement has prevailed on account of a wild man who was seen by several parties on the Lehigh mountain in the vicinity of what is known as the "Big Rock." The story was taken by many as a newspaper hoax, but that some one is hiding on the mountain who is either wild or an escaped lunatic, from some asylum, appears to be a fact that can not be disputed. On last Sunday a week several families from Allentown drove to our town, and in passing over the mountain, seen a miserable object of humanity coming out of the woods. He was covered with rags, which hung to him in shreds; long bushy hair covered his head and face, and upon seeing the approaching carriage he at once tried to hide his face by throwing his arm over his eyes. As soon as the carriage passed him he began to low in imitation of a cow, in a furious manner, and again disappeared in the woods. How he subsists or where he hides is unknown, but very likely he has his habitation in some cave among the rocks in the mountain. People in the vicinity say that his lowing or bawling is heard quite frequently, and he has become a sort of terror in the neighborhood.[20]

◆

The blackberry season is approaching and the Berks county newspapers have trotted out a wild man, "with a face, half human and half dog," who terrifies the women around Flourtown.[21]

◆

A Ghost Story.

We have had wonderful snake stories while the weather was warm; but of late I suppose he has been looking up winter quarters and left the outer world. But like Greeley we realize the days of misfortunes, cares and temptation have not closed. Mr. Nehemiah Cooper and wife with some friends were returning from Mt. Nebo church one night last week, and when near Wm. P Cooper's saw a strange monster at first the size of a bucket, but in a few seconds it became 12 or 15 feet high, 6 or 7 feet across the shoulders. The party, supposing it a trick of some one, at first commenced to pelt it with stones; but his ghostship stood the shock, advanced on the party, while they retreated to a place of safety. The only loss, I believe, is that Mount Nebo will lose part of its membership at night, unless there can be volunteers sufficient raised to hunt the monster down.[22]

◆

A wild man is said to be roaming over the country near Campbell's Mills. He was seen by a number of parties, who describe him as being a large, stout man, almost destitute of clothing, his only apparel being a shirt which has evidently seen better times.[23]

◆

— Mahaffy, Pa., reports a wild man who made his lair in a deserted log hut, within a hundred feet of a den of rattlesnakes, and spends his whole time wandering about in the mountain solitudes, avoiding his own kind as he would a plague.[24]

The Wild Man of Mahaffy.

A dispatch from Mahaffy to the Pittsburgh *Com.-Gazette* says: "The people of this village are trying to solve a mystery. On Saturday, May 26, a gentleman driving along the road leading from Curwensville to this place, noticed smoke issuing from a pine thicket on the south side of the river a mile below Mahaffy. In the center of the thicket is an old tumble down log stable, used years ago by lumbermen for their horses. The ground adjacent to the thicket is an open common used as a pasture for cattle. On Sunday last, while a Mr. Johnston was looking for his cow, he noticed a man suddenly bound out of the stable and make for the woods as if afraid to meet a fellow creature. On other occasions this same man has been seen but always fled like a wild animal when observed. Yesterday Squire W. W. McQuown and Emery Mahaffy made an investigation of the place and found in the old stable a rude bed made of hemlock boughs and a fire place a few feet from the couch, where the strange individual cooked his meals. No person was to be seen, however. The hermit had evidently noticed the approach of the party and escaped to the mountain a short distance back of his lonely habitation. A den of rattlesnakes, only a few hundred feet from his camp, which is the terror of the neighborhood, must certainly furnish weird music for the lone citizen. The hermit is a man about 40 years of age, of tall and commanding figure. His hair and beard are unkempt, and he looks as though he has been roughing it for months. *Who is he?* is the question the people of Mahaffy are anxious to have answered.[25]

LOST OR KIDNAPPED.

Mysterious Disappearance of Little Florence Hughes.

Friday forenoon Florence Hughes, the two-year-old daughter of John Hughes, an employee of the Bradford Oil Company, who lives on the Rutherford farm, was playing in that vicinity with two other children. The little one's playmates left her alone while they were seeking flowers in a clump of underbrush near by, and when they returned she was gone.

Mr. and Mrs. Hughes were immediately notified and instituted a rigorous search, but could find no trace of the missing one. All day long the fruitless search was kept up. In the evening a crowd started out from this city, swelling the number in the searching party to over 100.

Every nook and spot in the woods and fields within a radius of one mile was examined closely but without success. The lost babe could not be found. The parents are nearly distracted and have the keen sympathy of many friends in their trouble. It is believed the child has been kidnapped and stolen away. *The Era* contained an account of a supposed wild being, a few days ago, who has been seen in the locality of late, and it is now feared the loathsome wretch has spirited the child away to his lair in the hills. Major Adsitt, of the Bradford Oil Company, ordered the men employed under his direction to prosecute the search until a clue is found somewhere. These, together with a large band of volunteer searchers, spent the night diligently seeking for the missing child. At a late hour nothing had been heard from the missing one.

Florence is a handsome child. She wore Friday a checked gingham sailor suit; she has long, brown, curly hair, a round face, brown eyes and rosy cheeks and is stoutly built. Any information concerning her whereabouts will be joyfully received by the distracted parents.

No Trace of the Little One.

Rutherford, Pa., July 20. Florence, the little two-year-old child of John Hughes, who has been missing from home since 10 o'clock this morning, has not been found, although there were at least 200 men and boys with torches and lanterns scouring the woods all the evening. So far the search has been fruitless. It is thought that she may have been carried away by the wild man who has been seen by several in this locality recently. The parents are nearly frantic and earnestly request assistance to continue the search tomorrow morning. All who will kindly assist will please meet at J.T. Jones' boiler house, Rutherford Farm, at 8 p.m. sharp.

The Search Abandoned.

A party consisting of J.P. Taylor, Thomas Mills and two members of *The Era* staff visited the Rutherford district at 2 o'clock this morning and learned that no trace had been found of the lost child. A heavy fog hung over the woods and the search was abandoned till daylight.[26]

Some persons who have been drinking mountain dew, manufactured in the neighborhood of Nicktown, report that they met a wild man in the neighborhood of Mehaffey. They report him as being ten feet high, and covered in hair and his tracks in the sand measure 16 inches. That Nicktown whiskey must be terrible stuff. We imagine the men who originated the story are in training for campaign liars for Democratic newspapers. If they would take a few lessons from the editor of the Indiana Democrat, they might get situations promptly.[27]

For the past several days wild rumors have been floating about to the effect that some gigantic animal resembling a gorilla is running at large through the forests near Big Run. Several parties had reported seeing strange tracks in the mud at various places. At first no account was taken of it, but the reports came in so thickly that several prominent citizens of Big Run finally concluded to investigate the matter. Going to the places designated they were surprised to find the tracks more peculiar and gigantic than had been reported. They measured one of them and it proved to be a trifle over sixteen inches in length. It was wide at the toes and narrowed gradually toward the heel. Distinct marks of toes with long nails or claws were visible, suggesting the idea of a gorilla. The animal has not yet been sighted, but the oldest hunters acknowledge themselves completely at a loss to know to what species of created beings that wonderful foot belongs.[28]

THE GHOST OF CROWLEY.

Citizens Scared by an Unusual Animal in the Woods.

For several weeks past the citizens of Big Run and vicinity have been excited over the appearance of strange foot prints in the forest paths of Henderson township. The tracks were examined by the principle citizens of the place, who gazed upon them in blank amazement and recked not what to say. Though resembling in some degree a human foot print, the toes were too long, and the foot too wide in front and too narrow behind to belong to a man. Some light is thrown upon the identity of the strange creature by the testimony of George Depp, son of Bush Depp, of Clayville, who saw the monster with his own eyes. He was walking along the road in the woods, near the old Kramer oil well, when he saw, a few rods in front of him, a monster of hideous mein. It appeared to him to be a man, with long shaggy hair all over his body, with tremendous long arms , and an enormous mouth, filled with huge, white teeth. The sight for a moment almost chilled his blood. It was broad day light, and he could not be deceived. After recovering his self-possession Mr. Depp concluded he would make a detour of the woods and avoid any closer inspection of the monster. "I thought sure I had met the devil himself," said Mr. Depp. "This was over two weeks ago," he continues, "but I was afraid to say anything about it for fear people would think I was drunk or crazy, but when I heard everybody talking about those strange foot prints I concluded that I had seen the original." Mr. Depp is a perfectly reliable young man, not given to exaggeration, and he says he is willing to be qualified to the truth of the story. Many people seem to think it is the wild man seen about two months ago in the forests near Mahaffy. Our own idea is that it is the ghost of Mr. Crowley, the gorilla which recently died in New York City.[29]

———◆———

A wild man is among the people in the vicinity of Punxsutawny.[30]

———◆———

A Big Run Sensation.

A dispatch from Punxsutawny says: Big Run, a few miles above here, has a sensation. Tracks about 18 inches long are plentiful in the forest about the town, and people insist that a wild man is in the wilderness. The gigantic track is certainly to be seen, but what makes it is a mystery. It bears no resemblance to the track of any animal known hereabouts.[31]

———◆———

[1] *Harrisburg Telegraph* (Harrisburg, PA), January 3, 1881.
Besides the first appearance, in this book, of the term "gorilla" used to describe bigfoot creatures, this account notes several confrontations between the creature and dogs. Bigfoot have long been noted to kill, injure, and otherwise terrorize dogs. There are other accounts of this in this volume, both preceding and following this article. As with all things bigfoot *WHY* the creatures take issue with dogs comes down to guessing - educated or otherwise. Some people think they may simply be eating our canine companions; others believe it is because dogs can more easily detect a bigfoot's presence.

[2] *Reading Times* (Reading, PA), January 21, 1881.
"Catamount" is a general term applied to large wild cats, most often cougars. The word comes from "cat of the mountains". Interestingly, some people from rural regions of the southern U.S. have reported that they use the term "catamount" as a name for bigfoot creatures.

[3] *The Indiana Progress* (Indiana, PA), November 3, 1881.

[4] *Huntingdon Journal* (Huntingdon, PA), November 4, 1881.

[5] *The Spectator* (Hanover, PA), March 28, 1883.
Besides wild-men and gorillas, it seems bigfoot creatures in Pennsylvania were also sometimes described as some kind of man-bear hybrid creature. "A thing like a man, but hairy as a bear" or, as in this article, something with a "dual form of a man and a bear".

[6] *The Times* (Philadelphia, PA), July 7, 1883.

[7] *Harrisburg Daily Independent* (Harrisburg, PA), July 9, 1883.
This as well as the story above represent the somewhat rarer "wild woman" stories. This article is notable because of the missing woman - who may or may not have been the wild person in question - but as previously noted, some First Nations people say that bigfoot creatures will abduct people. There are strange modern missing persons cases in which bigfoot creatures are suspected as abductors. Though the author, David Paulides, maintains that he doesn't think bigfoot are responsible for the cases in his *Missing 411* series of books, there are several reports included in those volumes which mention things that certainly meet the description of bigfoot.

[8] *The Wellsboro Gazette* (Wellsboro, PA), July 17, 1883.

[9] *The Daily Republican* (Monogahela, PA), June 6, 1884.

[10] *Butler Citizen* (Butler, PA), June 11, 1884.

[11] *Dollar Weekly News* (Wilkes-Barre, PA), June 21, 1884.

[12] *The Columbian* (Bloomsburg, PA), July 18, 1884.

[13] *Pittsburgh Post-Gazette* (Pittsburgh, PA), August 26, 1884.

[14] *Dollar Weekly News* (Wilkes-Barre, PA), September 6, 1884.

[15] *Juniata Sentinel and Republican* (Mifflintown, PA), October 8, 1884.

[16] *Sunday News* (Wilkes-Barre, PA), December 28, 1884.

[17] *The Times* (Philadelphia, PA), December 30, 1884.

This article reads almost like a menu of bigfoot encounters: unearthly yells; stone throwing; a half-human, half-beast who frightens an armed and experienced hunter so much that he runs all the way home. The reporter's "solution" to the mystery, a young woman living in an old cabin, does not seem to fit with the rest of the details. Perhaps there was a young woman AND a bigfoot creature; perhaps the reporter was simply trying to come up with a "reasoned" explanation; or perhaps there really was a 25 year old woman who was scaring experienced hunters off of the mountain. If it is the latter, she must have been quite a sight to see!

[18] *Lancaster Daily Intelligencer* (Lancaster, PA), January 21, 1885.

[19] *The Hazleton Sentinel* (Hazleton, PA), June 5, 1885.

[20] *The Central News* (Perkasie, PA), June 18, 1885.

[21] *Lancaster Daily Intelligencer* (Lancaster, PA), July 10, 1885.

[22] *The Delta Herald* (Delta, PA), November 5, 1886.

There are reports of bigfoot creatures springing upright in a flash from a prone position - this may explain why the monster starts out the size of a "bucket". 12 or 15 feet is massive, even for a bigfoot - but I think it would be easy to overestimate a creature's size during such an encounter. One of the reasons I include this as a bigfoot sighting, besides the size of the creature reported, is the location. This report falls with a cluster of bigfoot sightings which all occurred within a few square miles but extend over many years - this report being the first that I know of - with other reports from 1972, 1978, and 2014. If you extend the location just a bit further many, many more bigfoot reports from the general Delta / Peach Bottom area can be documented over the years. I have visited the site of each of the reports mentioned in the cluster above - one could easily walk from one to the other - and Mt. Nebo Church is almost dead center of these sightings. Nehemiah Cooper and his wife are buried in the cemetery at Mt. Nebo Church.

[23] *The Indiana Progress* (Indiana, PA), May 9, 1888.

[24] *Wilkes-Barre Times Leader* (Wilkes-Barre, PA), June 6, 1888.

[25] *The Indiana Progress* (Indiana, PA), June 13, 1888.

[26] *Bradford Era* (Bradford, PA), July 21, 1888.
A very disturbing story of a missing child in conjunction with wild man sightings. This report reads like a number of the *Missing 411* cases. The child was left alone for a very short time and went missing without a trace - a vast search with a huge search party turns up no evidence - and the weather turns to interrupt the search (in this case, a heavy fog).

[27] *The Indiana Weekly Messenger* (Indiana, PA), August 1, 1888.

[28] *The Indiana Weekly Messenger* (Indiana, PA), October 3, 1888.

[29] *The Pittsburgh Press* (Pittsburgh, PA), October 12, 1888.

[30] *The Weekly Courier* (Connellsville, PA), October 12, 1888.

[31] *Bradford Era* (Bradford, PA), October 13, 1888.

V. HALF MAN AND HALF BEAST

1890 - 1899

A NUDE MAN AT LARGE

The Sight of Several Men Frightens Him and He Quickly Disappears. People of the Vicinity Excited.

New Holland, July 26. — Great excitement was created in the vicinity of this village yesterday by the appearance of an apparently wild man. He was first seen on the road near Bear's hotel, two miles west of this place. He was naked, and when he saw several men approaching he ran away. He was next seen on the Peters road, from which he went towards Intercourse and was last seen on the Old road near Christ church.

He is described as a large and muscular looking man, and his size will probably deter those who saw him from endeavoring to arrest him. He is a stranger in the neighborhood.

About a year ago a man of similar description appeared in this section and wandered about for days before he was apprehended. He was taken into court and his examination there proved him of unsound mind. He said in court that he was commanded by the spirits to take off his clothes, and their power over him was so great that he could not resist. He was sent to jail for a short time, and since then nothing has been heard of him. His description answers to that of the naked man noted above. Word was sent to the constables of Leacock and adjoining townships to be on the lookout for this party.[1]

---◆---

— West Grove people are hunting for a wild man, who lives in the woods nearby.[2]

---◆---

THE WILD WOMAN AGAIN.

Said to Have Been Seen on South Mountain by Berry-Pickers.

WOMELSDORF, August 1.

The wild woman who roamed over South Mountain near this place years ago it is reported has made her appearance again. One of a party from this place while picking huckleberries says he saw her.

"While going through a ravine," he said, "our attention was drawn to a peculiar noise on the incline above. We ventured near the spot and saw to our amazement an object in an almost nude condition, long hair grown over its face and body, and one arm and one leg shorter than the other. It was hanging on a vine suspended from a large tree, swinging to and fro as if humming a lullaby.

"Upon seeing us it leaped from tree to tree and was soon out of sight, chattering to itself as it disappeared."

The affair has caused considerable talk here and the matter will be further investigated.[3]

---◆---

The city of Erie, Pa., and the surrounding country is said to be infested by a wild creature, half man and half beast, which visits the hen roosts at night and kills the fowls, sucking their blood and leaving their carcasses on the ground. His record is between 500 and 600 dead fowls up to date.[4]

---◆---

The wild woman of the Womelsdorf Mountains, who has not been seen for a number of years, has again appeared in the mountains near Womelsdorf to frighten huckleberry pickers.[5]

---◆---

There is a wild man roaming the pathless woods of Allegheny. The residents in the vicinity of a strip of woods located in the Tenth ward are in fear of bodily harm for themselves and children, for it is there he has been making his habitation since Tuesday.[6]

MAN OF THE MOUNTAIN

HAS THE CHILDREN OF HYDE PARK FRIGHTENED

The Parents are Also Alarmed at the Reports That are Being Circulated and He May be Hunted Down.

Great excitement was caused last night by the report that the man who lives in a cave on the West Mountain and who is known as the "wild man" was chasing children upon the back avenues of this side. It was reported that he had killed a little girl on Everett avenue, but upon investigation it was found that there was no truth to the report. The residents are very much alarmed and keep their children in doors after dark. There is no doubt that if the "wild man" is caught he will be severely treated by the excited parents.[7]

Afraid of the Wild Man.

The Scranton chief of police has been appealed to for protection from a wild man who roams about the mountains near the city. He chases children and lived on vegetables from the farms. He is either an escaped convict or an escaped lunatic.[8]

WILD MAN AT LARGE

He is Said to be Terrorizing Citizens Near New Bedford.

It is claimed that a wild man is roaming about the woods near New Bedford and that women and even men are afraid to venture away from home alone. It is said that several parties have been made up to capture the wild man but so far they have been unsuccessful. The community is said to be greatly excited.[9]

Two colored boys, William George and Jeremiah Johnson, of Middleburg, three miles south of Greencastle, tell a strange story of having been chased by a wild man while in a wooded patch of road near that place on Saturday. Their story was incredulously received until Sunday morning when a man by the name of Thomas rushed into town with the story of a wild flight from a red-bearded giant with a club. His description of the man and his fright convinced many that the boys account might be true. A party has been searching for the man, but without success.[10]

———◆———

A wild man, or one demented, has been discovered on the ridge in the vicinity of Winger's sawmill. The man is only half clothed, and wanders through the brush aimlessly. He never ventures in the clear land. A party of hunters came upon the individual, and like a deer, he bounded away and was lost in the thicket. It is supposed that the man escaped from some country home. An effort will be made to capture him.[11]

———◆———

A giant wild man is said to be running at large through the wilds of Potter county and the feats which he easily performs are of the hair-raising variety. The Galeton Gazette tells some horrible tales about him but neglects to add an affidavit to the story as a guarantee of good faith.[12]

———◆———

A Wild Man in Potter County.

A giant wild man is terrorizing the inhabitants of Potter county according to the Galeton Gazette. He is described as giant in size with high, broad shoulders, extraordinary long arms, large head, and his whole body is covered with thick, dark hair. He is probably the same wild man that was reported as having been seen over near Hull's last spring. His appearance has set the county in a commotion.[13]

———◆———

Some people near Galeton, about ten days since, were frightened by what they supposed was a wild man of immense stature all covered with hair. It has since transpired that the supposed wild man was a large bear walking on its hind feet as they frequently do. Tom Harrington's fertile brain and ready pen will make Galeton and vicinity noted for its many curiosities.[14]

———————◆———————

It is reported that a wild man is terrorizing the inhabitants of the West Branch valley. He is described as giant in size, with high broad shoulders, very long arms, large head, and his whole body covered with thick, dark hair.[15]

———————◆———————

A Wild Man Captured.

The statement was made a few days ago that a wild man was terrorizing the people of Potter county by his presence. Last Friday the man was captured by a posse of nearly 100 men. The man was first discovered by some women wild berrying. He was not afraid of women but would flee at the presence of a man. Wonderful stories are told about the marvelous strength of the captured man. He is said to be nearly seven feet in height and his body is covered with long hair. Flowing locks, two feet in length, hung down his back and his hands are said to resemble long bird-like claws.[16]

———————◆———————

— Mr. D.F. Manning, of Hammersly's Fork, writes us that the story of the capture of the "wild man," and that his name was Bodine Brooks, is all a "fake." He writes further, "I saw Bodine Brooks yesterday at his home. His brother has the care of him and he looks well kept. He has no more hair on him than the average man who wears whiskers and has a full head of hair." Mr. Manning thinks some newspaper scribbler must have been badly taken in on the "wild man" story.[17]

———————◆———————

— Sometime since we pronounced the *Galeton Gazette*'s wild man a bear. Then comes the Wellsboro *Republican* with a wonderful cock and bull story that Bodine Brooks, of Leidy, Clinton county, Pa., who has been demented since his birth, and made his escape from confinement and was terrorizing the people near Galeton. We have known of this terrible wild man, Brooks, since 1857, and knew that he was not the dangerous demon pictured by the *Republican*. To make doubly sure, we wrote to a gentleman who lives less than two miles from said Brooks, enclosing a copy of the wonderful story concocted by the fertile brain of the Wellsboro scribe, and he says Brooks has not escaped to the woods, but is docile and peaceable, although in warm weather he objects to wearing a superfluous quantity of clothing, neither is his body covered with long hair; his head covering is not matted. In closing, our correspondent says, "Who ever made the false statement in the Wellsboro *Republican* ought to be made to correct it." We trust that this will have a tendency to stop some of the would-be imitators of Baron Munchausen, as such yarns gotten up can not help but effect the feelings of the relatives of the unfortunates.[18]

──────◆──────

A TWO-HEADED GIRL.

Tom Harrington Discovers One on the Potato Creek Road.

Truthful Tom Harrington of the Galeton Gazette, says there is a two-headed girl living on the Emporium end of the Potato Creek road, on North creek. She is 13 years old and her faces are very pretty. She is accomplished in music and sings a duet by herself, one voice being a soprano and the other an alto. She is brunette and is unusually bright. Her parents, Mr. and Mrs. Lewis, have been offered large sums by show people for the girl's services as a museum attraction, but they refuse all offers from such people and are much devoted to their very interesting daughter.

In the same issue of his valuable journal Mr. Harrington tells about a crop of buckwheat near Galeton that is doing nicely. Many of the buckwheat stalks are six feet high. Considering the long drouth and the prevalence of prohibition laws in Potter county, this buckwheat takes high rank among the record breakers of '94.

Mr. Harrington's wild man, spoken of recently in *The Era*, is still at large and the tin mines of Potter county which he discovered are cutting quite a figure in nearby newspapers.[19]

──────◆──────

HALLSTEAD'S WILD WOMAN

Thought to be a relative of the Binghamton Herald's Wild Man Who Eats Horses and Picks His Teeth with a Crowbar.

Hallstead, Pa., Aug. 2 — Our inhabitants are terribly frightened over the appearance of a wild woman, said to be the wife of the wild man seen near Hancock, and many will not go out after dark. She was at Susquehanna on Friday evening after the men had quit work, and went to a machine shop and removed with perfect ease a balance wheel. She mounted it and rode toward this place as easily as many can ride a bicycle. She was met near Smoky Hollow by a peddler with a horse. She dismounted from her balance wheel and possessed the same knack as the wild man did in dislocating the neck of the horse, as with one jerk she broke its neck. With a slight wave of her hand she rendered the poor peddler unconscious. She then dragged the horse to the woods, where its bones were found today, showing that she had eaten the horse. The peddler recovered from his severe blow, and while sitting down thinking over his troubles he heard two men coming in the darkness; and these proved to be Aaron Rhinhart and Jason Melody, who gave the alarm. The wild woman was not pursued until morning, when a large crowd started in pursuit, and looking over the ground where she had last been seen immense tracks were discovered, showing the size of her foot, the toes of which measured six inches and one in diameter. They followed the trail the best they could. As they got near Turkey Hill they saw to their astonishment a pile of rattlesnake skins, showing that the creature eats snakes as well as horses. They returned on Saturday, but had not seen her. It is rumored she is in a cave near Mt. Manotome, but no one dare go to find out. Officers Higgins and Hogan say they will catch her yet, if it is in their power.

In an interview the peddler today informed the correspondent that the woman was about 8½ feet tall, and he thought weighed about 500 pounds. He said that instead of large sleeves, her arms were covered by a heavy growth of hair, which, he said, would be the style in a few years.[20]

Reports are rife in parts of Manayunk that a wild man has been seen roaming in that region who is nude, long-haired and ferocious in action, but no one knows whence he came and where he is going.[21]

A wild man has been discovered on the Chestnut Ridge, four or five miles south of Boliver. His clothing consists of trousers worn off at the knees and an overcoat torn almost to shreds. He wore a slouch hat pulled down over a shaggy face, his hair falling in tangled locks on his shoulders. A searching party went to hunt the man. He was seen by the party, but like a flash he bounded away and was lost among the rocks and brush. It is believed the mysterious man is Brookamire, who killed his father-in-law in Indiana county two years ago, and disappeared.[22]

◆

Brookamire Discovered Again.

Word comes from Greensburg that a wild man has been discovered on the Chestnut Ridge, four or five miles south of Bolivar. A day or two ago, James Shirley, a citizen of that neighborhood, while strolling along the foot of the mountains saw a queer-looking individual rapidly climbing the mountainside as though making an effort to run away from some one. His clothing consisted of pantaloons worn off at the knees and an overcoat torn almost into threads. He wore a slouch hat pulled down over a shaggy face, his hair falling in tangled locks on his shoulders.

A searching party was organized, and, headed by Mr. Shirley and Charles Johnson, on Wednesday made a tour of the Ridge in search of the man. He was seen by the party, but only for a moment. Like a flash the man bounded away and was lost among the brush. It is the opinion of some that the mysterious man is Brookamire, who killed his father-in—law in Indiana county two years ago and who disappeared after the murder. The presence of the strange individual has caused a good deal of excitement in the neighborhood. Another effort will be made to discover his hiding place.[23]

◆

A wild man in the woods is terrorizing the natives of Bolivar and vicinity.[24]

◆

There is an alleged "wild man" terrorizing the people of Norristown, daily and nightly and there is no one brave enough to capture the unfortunate creature. He is searching for a wife.[25]

◆

Searching for a Wild Man.

Ligonier, Pa., June 4. — Accounts from the mountains near Nero, Florence, and Bolivar go to show that the wild man seen last winter is still in the woods. On Tuesday he was seen by two men, but immediately disappeared in a dark thicket. It is thought that the man is Brookamire, who murdered his father-in-law in that section two years ago, and a crowd is searching for him.[26]

A wild man in semi-nude condition and having very long hair was seen running through the streets of Brownsville on Saturday night, and about half past eleven o'clock. The report is verified by several residents.[27]

A gorilla supposed to have escaped from a circus is roaming over the York county hills.[28]

As some women from upper Farview street were picking berries on the Fallbrook mountain last Friday, they met with an experience which will have a tendency to keep them off the mountain for some time to come. There were four persons in the party and they had no male protectors. They reached the mountain and were picking berries but a short time when they heard a suppressed cough from some brush that was close by. They kept very diligent watch on that bush when suddenly there burst from it and bearing down on them at a rapid pace a man stark naked. His eyes were flashing fire and he had every appearance of being insane. In his mad rush to reach the women his foot caught in a root and he fell heavily to the ground. Then the berry pickers seemed to awaken from their terror-stricken condition and dropping their pails and sunbonnets, they rushed off at break neck speed. Through bush and over stones they ran and came out on the clearing almost dead from excitement and exhausted from the long run. They reached home more dead than alive and gave account of their adventure. A number of men from that section left yesterday for the mountain where they scoured the woods but could find no trace of the wild man.[29]

SHE IS A WILD WOMAN

Strange Creature Found in a Mountain Fastness.

SHE RAN FROM A HUNTER

DISCOVERED CROONING OVER A RUDE FIRE IN HER DESOLATE CAVE — PEOPLE CANNOT CATCH HER.

Laporte, Pa., Nov. 27 — A hunter named Haffa, who returned a day or two ago from the Elk Creek and Little Loyalsock regions, tells a startling story about a wild woman whom he encountered in a hemlock forest, fully ten miles away from human habitation.

Haffa was waiting on a deer "run" while his companion sauntered across the ridge in the direction that a doe which they raised had taken. As Haffa stood listening intently for the breaking of twigs under the deer's feet he was profoundly surprised to hear the notes of a song in clear, feminine voice. The sounds seemed to come from the direction of a ledge of rocks about two rods away.

It was a weird, strange song, but the voice was so sweet that the hunter could do naught but stand and listen. Literally at a loss to explain the strange affair and half frightened at having heard the uncanny song. Haffa at first was impelled to hurry away. Peering in the direction of the rock ledge he could discern a gray streak of smoke curling up between the trees, and he concluded that a party of campers must be "bunked" there during their hunting expedition.

Making his way through an almost impenetrable thicket of laurel and ground hemlock that hemmed in a small stream between himself and the ledge of rocks Haffa was treated to a greater surprise than was the song when it broke upon his ears.

There, under a projecting rock that formed a roof, alongside a small fire, stood a woman whose disheveled hair and tattered gown gave her the appearance of a hag. She was evidently roasting something over the fire, for every now and then she poked the embers with a stick, as though distributing the heat over a given surface. She was a woman about 40 years, quite tall and masculine in build, with a face wholly unprepossessing — even repulsive.

The woman had drawn

heavy sticks and stood them together against the shelving rock, forming a sort of rude, hovel-like structure, for the covering of which she used strips of bark. All the while she was cooking over the smoking embers she kept humming that weird, odd tune, much like the song a witch might sing over her pot of herbs.

She was bare headed, her matted, coarse hair hanging in disheveled rolls over her back and shoulders. Her gown was torn in strings about the breast and shoulders, and at the bottom it hung in rags about her feet. The shoes she wore were evidently men's shoes — heavy and coarse. and showed the effects of much wear and tear over the rocks and mountains.

Hidden as he was, back of a clump of ground hemlocks, Haffa had an obstructed view of the hideous creature, and he watched her fully twenty minutes. Suddenly, in shifting positions, his foot slipped, and coming in contact with a half rotten stick, snapped the bough in twain. Quick as a flash, the woman straightened up, ceased her humming and scanned the woods about her.

Haffa says she looked more like a wild beast than a human being as she stood glaring into space, her great, piercing black eyes shifting from side to side, and her attitude one of intense excitement and strain.

Haffa gave a low whistle. The woman, evidently having grown suspicious, began moving about and, shading her eyes with her hands, looked into the recesses of the forest. Haffa then straightened up and advanced toward the creature, but the sight of him sent her screaming down the hillside like one possessed of devils. She was out of sight in a minute, not even stopping long enough to see whether she was being pursued.

Haffa examined the rude shelter against the rocks. That the woman had slept there was unmistakable, for the bed of hemlock boughs showed the impression of her body. Three potatoes in the wood ashes at the fireside showed what the woman had been cooking. Her abode beneath the rocks gave evidences of having been used for some time, as the brushes were trampled and dead.

A slightly worn path led off in the direction that the woman had taken, but after following this a rod or two it ended abruptly at the bank of the stream. Here was found a cup shaped vessel made of birch bark, and which evidently had been used by the woman as a drinking cup.[30]

A Wild Man of Clarion

Oil City, Pa., April 15 — From Edenburg, Clarion County, comes a story of an insane man running at large in the woods near that place. A man, whose identity is unknown, has been seen several times near the roads leading to Edenburg, clad in unkempt garments and in a generally disheveled appearance. Efforts to approach him are only rewarded by him running away, and he seems to have an aversion to meeting any person, and residents of the county nearby are not making any attempt to mix up with the recluse, who is said to make his home in a cave in the woods.[31]

CHASED BY A WILD MAN.

Pottstown, Pa., July 22 — A wild man is at bay in Sprigles Valley near Saratoga. For the past four weeks or longer children playing about Richards Wood have been disturbed in their innocent pleasure by hideous cries like that of a catamount, and occasionally the youthful groups come to their homes and tell stories of a man who runs after them trying to catch them.

These stories were generally discredited by older persons until Tuesday, when the wild man gave chase to a daughter of Levi Oxenfeld. He was entirely nude, and yelled like a madman. The child made for home with all her might, and the last she saw of him was in an oat field near by. Mr. Oxenford and his father-in-law, John P. Koppel, at once made a search but nothing could be seen of the fellow.[32]

WHAT IS IT?

Strange Beast Said to Have Been Seen Near Coal Valley.

Mckeesport, Sept. 16 — The people of Coal valley are panic-stricken over a strange animal that has been seen in Wilson's woods, a 400-acre tract back of the village. Wild ravines and deserted coal pits were the only attractions in the woods until a few days ago. John Wilhelm, whose house is on the edge of the woods, was the first man to see the monster. It came up to his porch a few mornings ago and looked at the window. In appearance it seemed to be an ape or a very old man covered with hair. It walked on its hind legs and seemed very nimble on its feet. Wilhelm was going to shoot it, but before he got his gun it bounded over the railing of the porch and disappeared in the woods.

Oliver Payne, a dairyman, also saw the strange thing. He had gone out to the woods to look for a stray cow when he noticed the strange looking monster coming toward him. Payne took to his heels in the opposite direction. The monstrosity has also been seen by William Chambers, another farmer.

The people at Coal valley are organizing an expedition and will try and capture the beast or whatever it may be.[33]

UNUSUAL GAME

Farmer Pettis Went After Foxes, but Found a Wild Man Instead.

A farmer named Pettis recently went fox hunting over the range, near Elk mountain, in Susquehanna county. Hearing his dog barking loudly on the opposite side of the mountain, he went there, thinking he had bayed some large animal. To his astonishment he discovered that the dog had at bay a man on the cliff of a large rock just above.

The man was of giant mold, with long hair and whiskers. His clothes appeared to be made of skins and patches of cloth. In his hand he carried a long, crooked cane. He wore no hat. His sleeves were worn almost to ribbons, leaving his arms exposed.

When Farmer Pettis addressed this stranger, he answered with an unintelligible gibberish, and finally began to yell. The stranger then climbed the rocks and was lost to view.

The farmer followed the trail, but it was lost in a road used by teamsters.

For several years there have been stories of such a personage having been seen upon the mountain, and it is believed that he occupies a cave somewhere upon the range, which is the highest point in Pennsylvania.[34]

AN AWFUL POSSIBILITY.

Whitney has discovered a wild man on Elk mountain. If Whitney should go among the farmers of Elk mountain and they knew who he was, he would think there were more wild men than one in this vicinity — Dundaff correspondent *Forest City News*. Can it be possible that the

Dundaff writer is also roaming over the mountains?[35]

FOREST CITY.

According to a veracious inhabitant of Elkdale, a wild man has his stamping ground in a region of Elk Mountain and Crystal lake. He appeared to a party of wood choppers recently, performed a series of Delsartean movements and suddenly with something less than twenty feet bounds buried himself in the "dense underbrush."[36]

An Elkdale resident insists that there is a wild man loose in the forest near Elk mountain, and that on a recent occasion he was seen by workmen in the woods near Crystal lake. The writer adds that "with gestures and rapid strides he soon disappeared in the dense underbrush." A wild man who has this double means of disappearing will be a difficult customer to catch. Rapid striding is hard enough to follow, but it is taking a mean advantage of civilized men to add gestures as an additional method of locomotion. For this heretofore unheard-of proceeding, if for nothing else, the Elk mountain wild man ought to be suppressed.[37]

The Elkdale correspondent of the *Forest City News* says the wild man was again seen near Crystal Lake a few days since. The verification of my first report is very gratifying.[38]

A wild man has been seen on Peter's Mountain from time to time by creditable witnesses, and he is described as being without shoes or shirt, the repulsive face covered with hair and the hair of his head hanging far down on the back in wild confusion. He has been addressed by different persons, but replies to all questions by guttural growls and flees with surprising swiftness, shunning human companionship. The smoke of his camp fire has been frequently seen by different parties hunting chestnuts. The creature is supposed to be an escaped lunatic.[39]

Wild Man on Twolick Hills.

A wild man who has been roaming over Twolick hills for a couple weeks, has struck consternation into the hearts of many of the residents of that locality and disconcerted the numerous berry pickers who gather fruit from the bushes on the hills. The man is large and strong, and his only apparel is a pair of boots and a coffee sack over the upper part of his body. When he meets a man in the woods he at once runs away, but his conduct when he meets a woman, is different. There are a number of vacant shanties on the hills and he takes up his abode in one of them during the night and feeds on green corn and berries. His name is said to be Akefield and he is a brother of the man killed on the P. R. R. a few weeks ago. The authorities will be requested to look after him.[40]

―――――◆―――――

The wild man who has been roaming over Twolick hills for some weeks has not been captured.[41]

―――――◆―――――

Our "Wild Man" Story as It Travels

"Down along the Indiana county line, where panthers and lions and sundry other wild beasts have been seen during the past year, they now report a wild man. They say he has been seen by berry pickers on Twolick mountain, and that he wears boots and a coffee sack. When discovered accidentally, he breaks away through the brush like a wild animal. It is said he is a brother of a man killed on the Pennsylvania Railroad weeks ago. He is supposed to be insane and is not thought to be armed. Constables are trying to catch him, but he is very elusive." — *Pittsburgh Times*.[42]

―――――◆―――――

CHASED BY A WILD-MAN

Section of Chester County Stirred Up by Alarming Reports

POTTSTOWN, Sept. 27 — People living in the vicinity of Coventryville, Chester county, report that a wild man is roaming the Chestnut Hills and delights in frightening women and children. Last evening he chased Miss Anna McFarland for over a mile. It is believed that he is an escaped lunatic.[43]

[1] *Lancaster Daily Intelligencer* (Lancaster, PA), July 26, 1890.

[2] *Harrisburg Telegraph* (Harrisburg, PA), October 24, 1890.

[3] *The Times* (Philadelphia, PA), August 2, 1891.
A strange looking creature indeed - and one that leaps away from tree to tree without problem. While located in the same area as the previous Wolmelsdorf wild-woman reports, there was no previous mention of the asymmetrical limbs as reported on this creature. This would lead me to think it is a different entity. Note the "chattering" as the creature retreated. Bigfoot speech, if indeed it is speech, is often reported as sounding like "chatter".

[4] *Olean Democrat* (Olean, NY), August 6, 1891.
Here we have a blood sucking chicken-killer report. Modern reports of bigfoot killing chickens for their blood are not unheard of (in fact my book, *Beyond the Seventh Gate*, has a report of a bigfoot creature sucking the blood from chickens dating from the 1970s in York County, PA).

[5] *The New Oxford Item* (New Oxford, PA), August 7, 1891.

[6] *Pittsburgh Dispatch* (Pittsburgh, PA), October 11, 1891.

[7] *The Scranton Republican* (Scranton, PA), September 9, 1893.

[8] *Wilkes-Barre Semi-Weekly Record* (Wilkes-Barre, PA), September 15, 1893.

[9] *The New Castle News* (New Castle, PA), February 6, 1894.

[10] *Standard-Sentinel* (Hazleton, PA), March 14, 1894.

[11] *The Pittsburgh Press* (Pittsburgh, PA), April 2, 1894.

[12] *Bradford Era* (Bradford, PA), August 13, 1894.

[13] *Loch Haven Express* (Loch Haven, PA), August 24, 1894.

[14] *McKean County Miner* (Smithport, PA), August 24, 1894.

[15] *The Bradford Star* (Towanda, PA), August 30, 1894.

[16] *Loch Haven Express* (Loch Haven, PA), August 31, 1894.
Could it be that a bigfoot creature was captured in Pennsylvania?

There are a few accounts of the creatures being captured over time, but it is very rare. The description of this wild man seems to indicate, however, that the snide (and improbable) claim from the *McKean County Miner* (above) that the creature was an upright walking bear was incorrect.

[17] *Wellsboro Agitator* (Wellsboro, PA), September 5, 1894.

[18] *McKean County Miner* (Smithport, PA), September 14, 1894.

[19] *Bradford Era* (Bradford, PA), September 17, 1894.

The above three articles are an example of the kind of back-and-forth "debunking" prevalent in newspapers at the time. Any reporting of the unusual was called into question and ridiculed by other papers. This, of course, still happens in modern times. Here we have the wild man identified by name, thereby "solving" the case (yet again) as a normal, albeit hairy human. This resolution is countered with the information that the man in question is neither wild nor hairy. Finally, we have an article questioning the reporter of another paper which ends with the information that the wild man is still at large.

[20] *The Scranton Tribune* (Scranton, PA), August 3, 1895.

What to make of this strange story? A wild woman riding atop a balance wheel is a bit of a lighthearted image, but then the story takes a dark turn as the horse's neck is broken and the peddler attacked. The creature seems to fit the description of a bigfoot: the height, weight, hirsute state, and behavior - sans balance wheel riding - all seem to match up with other bigfoot reports. The attempt at humor in the last paragraph - my guess an addition of the reporter's and not a quote from the man who was attacked - noting that "hairy arms" would be the style for women in a few years makes me question the balance-wheel-riding part of the article as well. Was the reporter trying to inject levity into an otherwise dark and strange story?

[21] *Harrisburg Daily Independent* (Harrisburg, PA), August 27, 1895.

[22] *Warren Evening Democrat* (Warren, PA), November 11, 1895.

[23] *Indiana Weekly Messenger* (Indiana, PA), November 13, 1895.

[24] *The Ledger* (Warren, PA), November 15, 1895.

The above three articles most likely refer to a human, but the Chestnut Ridge is rife with modern bigfoot reports and other strangeness, so I thought it pertinent to include these stories.

[25] *Harrisburg Daily Independent* (Harrisburg, PA), January 6, 1896.

[26] *Pittsburgh Post-Gazette* (Pittsburgh, PA), June 5, 1896.
   It looks like Brookamire or whoever / whatever this wild man was, is still alive and haunting the Chestnut Ridge six months later.

[27] *Evening Herald* (Shenandoah, PA), June 29, 1896.

[28] *Harrisburg Daily Independent* (Harrisburg, PA), June 30, 1896.

[29] *The Scranton Republican* (Scranton, PA), July 28, 1896.

[30] *Sunday News* (Wilkes-Barre, PA), November 29, 1896.
   The clothes and use of fire would most likely disqualify this wild woman as a bigfoot creature. However, I will note that there have been modern bigfoot reports of the creatures wearing ragged clothes. These reports are exceedingly rare and often ignored by the strict ape-in-the-woods bigfoot researcher crowd because they do not "fit" in with their beliefs about the creatures. Likewise, some bigfoot researchers as well as some First Nations people have reported that bigfoot can use fire, but that they use it very rarely and secretively - knowing that it is a certain giveaway should anyone see the light or smoke. All of that noted, who can say if the subject of this article was a feral human, a type of bigfoot creature, or something else entirely?

[31] *Pittsburgh Post-Gazette* (Pittsburgh, PA), April 16, 1897.

[32] *The Wilkes-Barre News* (Wilkes-Barre, PA), July 23, 1897.

[33] *The Pittsburgh Press* (Pittsburgh, PA), September 16, 1897.

[34] *The Gazette* (York, PA), February 13, 1898.

[35] *The Scranton Tribune* (Scranton, PA), March 9, 1898.

[36] *The Scranton Tribune* (Scranton, PA), April 9, 1898.
   Francois Delsarte developed a method of expressive movements for actors. The term "Delsartean" applies to this teaching. It was sometimes misunderstood in America to be a form of gymnastic movements and often devolved into rather melodramatic poses on the part of actors trained in the "Delsartean" method. We can only guess at the dramatic and /or gymnastic expressions performed by the "wild man" in this article - but a leap of near 20 feet would be incredibly impressive for any mere human, be they actor, gymnast, or feral man.

[37] *The Scranton Republican* (Scranton, PA), April 9, 1898.

[38] *The Scranton Tribune* (Scranton, PA), April 13, 1898.

[39] *Harrisburg Telegraph* (Harrisburg, PA), October 22, 1898.

[40] *The Indiana Weekly Messenger* (Indiana, PA), August 2, 1899.

[41] *The Indiana Weekly Messenger* (Indiana, PA), August 16, 1899.

[42] *The Indiana Weekly Messenger* (Indiana, PA), August 23, 1899.

[43] *The Philadelphia Inquirer* (Philadelphia, PA), September 28, 1899.

VI. A BLACK-BEARDED GHOUL-FACED THING

1900 - 1909

Discovered a Wild Man.

Newspaper correspondents at Cumberland have had much fun all week writing accounts of an alleged wild man who was found in a cave near the mountain base at Pen-Mar. It is not alleged that the poor old man is dangerous, but he is described as wild looking, with shaggy hair, bags tied to his feet instead of wearing shoes. He lives in a cave on a rock path, and spends most of his time sleeping by a fire built on the rock.[1]

◆

Jacob Wilson, a farm hand at John Q. Fertig's, with several others, who were engaged in hauling timber from Peter's Mountain, report as having discovered a wild man in the woods a few days ago. The unusual loud noise in the bushes suddenly terrorized the men, and they immediately prepared themselves for an attack with some ferocious animal. As the strange object drew nearer they discovered it was a wild man, with scarcely any clothing to cover his body. The men fled a short distance, and when they discovered that they were not pursued, they returned for their axes, and then left the place, the wild man, in the meantime, having disappeared.²

Shot at Wild Man.

The supposed wild man who has been terrorizing the residents of Mifflin and O'Hara townships has again made his appearance. Two shots were fired at the mysterious individual a few days ago by Harry Reed on the Payne farm, but did not take effect.³

Kennett Square has a "wild man in the woods" scare.⁴

TO HUNT A WILD MAN

Peculiar Spectacle Seen on the Boulevard Yesterday.

CHASED BUT DISAPPEARED

Police will Scour the District This Morning for a Demented Man who has Frightened a Number of Visitors in That section — Was Seen Yesterday by a Number of Persons.

A hunt for a "wild man" is promised bright and early today, on the Elmhurst boulevard. Many complaints have been made by children as well as grown up persons during the past few days of the conduct of a scantily dressed man who has been roaming through the brush adjoining the boulevard. It was thought that they were the antics of some drunken man. Yesterday afternoon, however, a prominent resident of the West Side, accompanied by his wife, while driving along the boulevard below the speedway, were startled to see a most peculiar specimen of humanity resting on a large stone about 100 feet away. It seemed to be a woman crouching as if in great pain. The whole form, however, was covered with a tattered shawl. Driving a little distance the West sider saw two young men who were walking ahead. He asked them if they had noticed the unnatural spectacle and they replied in the negative, but became so interested that they retraced their steps in the direction pointed out.

They succeeded in locating the shawl and the form it enveloped, but not in capturing it. When they arrived within shouting distance they gave a warning yell, and were afterwards too stupefied to run for a few seconds. The shawl was flung to the air and a man almost nude fled through the brush. They followed him but he seemed to have supernatural means of escape, being quickly lost to view. He was seen again running down the D. L. & W. tracks and entering the tunnel where others joined in the chase, but with no success.

His yells were heard at a great distance and were quite demoniacal. Chief Robling was notified last night and will detail a squad of men to scour the district this morning.

It is thought that the "wild man" is demented. His appearance is most fantastic, the hair being long and matty, while his finger nails appear to revel in a year's growth.[5]

---◆---

THE WILD MAN AGAIN

He Appeared Before and Frightened Two Dunmore Ladies.

Chief of Police Robling was notified yesterday by two ladies living in Dunmore, that they had seen the wild man of the mountains, near the Speedway hotel on the boulevard. They claimed that while passing along about 9:30 o'clock they saw a man only partially clothed, dogging their footsteps. He gave them a great fright and steps will now be taken by Chief Robling to discover the whereabouts of the man of mystery.

This was the first official notification that the police received, although vague rumors have been in the wind the past two days regarding some wild creature on the mountain. A thorough search will be made and it is likely in a day or two the mystery will be solved.[6]

---◆---

CHIEF SAYS THE MAN BELONGS TO DUNMORE

Is Not Afraid to Tackle the Wild Man of the Boulevard — But He Keeps Clear of His Territory.

The "wild man" of the Boulevard is apparently not demented after all. On the other hand, he is a most methodical crank. He knows the city line to an eighth of an inch, but never steps over it. He gives his performances within the borough of Dunmore, knowing full well that if he stepped on Scranton territory his career would be ended right there and then. For that reason he patronizes the borough and in the language of Chief Robling: "It's now up to the Dunmore police to arrest him."

Complaints were made yesterday to Chief Robling regarding the man who lives, eats, and sleeps in the bush near the Speedway. There is no truth to the rumor that the Races, Carnival, Grand Tournament, and Clam Bake of the City club tomorrow afternoon is to be abandoned owing to the proximity of the "wild man." It would not be abandoned even if the leprous Chinaman from Olyphant were let loose there.

On the other hand, some of the members have suggested a "wild man" hunt as a feature of the carnival to be led by Chairman Bedford with the two lion cubs from Nay Aug Park and Dr. Hill's bar. The members will be disappointed if the police arrest the wild man in the meantime and they hope that he will not become forgetful and step over the city line until the lions and bear have had a show.[7]

TERRIBLE PLIGHT OF A MAD WOMAN

Nearly Nude, She Runs at Large in Mountains Near Altoona.

Altoona, July 20.

A wild woman, almost naked and fearfully emaciated by prolonged exposure was seen by three Frugality miners, who were returning from work over the Allegheny today.

The unfortunate creature, at the sight of the men, fled like a deer into the mountain thickets, where she eluded the miners, who thought to capture her.

The woman is probably Mrs. Richard Kellar, of Frugality, who escaped from the home of relatives some weeks ago while insane.

Hundreds of people have searched for her since, but no trace of her whereabouts was discovered until today.[8]

---◆---

SAW THE WILD MAN

Brave Providence Boys Chased Him on the Boulevard.

Ernest Salsman and James Shaffer, two boys residing in Providence, were the heroes in that section of the city last night. They were picking berries near the Bird's Eye pond when they saw the "wild man" sitting in the brush. At their approach he fled and they gave him chase into the woods but, like the police, failed to capture him.

They described his appearance in vivid language and became so enthusiastic that a proposal is on foot to organize a company of North End boys to hunt the Wild Man of the Boulevard.[9]

---◆---

The wild man who has been frightening West side people has made his appearance on College hill. He chased two girls up College avenue, the other night, when I. R. Moore came to the rescue and gave the "wild man" a run for his money, until the latter disappeared along the abandoned mill race.[10]

---◆---

The wild (?) man made his appearance on College avenue for the second time, Tuesday night, and frightened two girls. The wild man is due to receive a load of buckshot as a number of citizens who love to hunt wild game are on his trail.[11]

---◆---

JUST FOR FUN

A Communication From the Wild Man.

Editor of the Evening rekord,

der sir — thare has bed a good eal said about me scarin girls on the streets and calling me a wilde man i onley do it fun. onley the homeley girls is chaste cause the pritty girls stay to home i chaste some the other nite an every last one of them was to homeley for enny use, I alwaos like pritty girls but I cant find enny on the street after ate oclock, if they be they will git chaste by me

yours truley

the Wilde man[12]

WILD MAN KEEPS WOMEN OF QUIET LITTLE TOWN IN STATE OF TERROR

TAMAQUA, Oct. 15 — The women of the little town of Coaldale are being terrorized by a supposed wild man and many of them are afraid to venture from their homes. Miss Lettie Earley, a public school teacher, while on her way home through the woods, was approached by an individual almost nude, whose head and face were covered with a coarse growth of hair, and whose expression was that of a maniac.

Miners approaching frightened the object away. The men gave chase, but the object was too nimble-footed and has thus far eluded capture. Numerous women and children have been chased by him, and searching parties are out.[13]

THEY FEAR A WILD MAN

He is Dressed in Black and Has a Bowing Acquaintance With Trees.

Mt. Penn has a mystery. The farmers living on the near side are startled and mystified by the figure of a demented man who is seen with a curious square package in his hand, and who pauses before a large tree and makes a low bow before it and then suddenly runs to it and butts his head against it with all his might. He disappears like magic whenever chase is made.

The man was seen only during the last few days. (unreadable text)...black with a collar. He always carries the mysterious package. No one has been near enough to describe... (unreadable). He is said by the farmers to be about (unreadable) years of age.

(unreadable) Detective John Smith searched all day yesterday afternoon and last evening for the man but without success. His bowing to the trees is supposed to be a religious hallucination.

The search will be continued as the farmers' families are afraid to walk away alone, through fear of meeting the stranger.[14]

Wild Man of Fulton County.

MCCONNELLSBURG, Pa., Nov. 23 — The farmers living on Mount Penn are greatly alarmed over the appearance of a wild man. Detectives are searching for him. The farmers say that the mysterious man carries a curious square package in his hand, pauses before a large tree, makes a low bow before it, and then butts his head against it. He disappears like magic when chased. His trousers are fringed above the knees and his coat is without sleeves. His hair is long, coming down over his shoulders.[15]

◆

Fulton has a wild man who lives in the woods.[16]

◆

Wild Man Said to be About

The farmers living on the southern slope of the Conewago hills, in the vicinity of Hill church, near Colebrook, are said to be greatly disturbed over the antics of a so called wild man. They say the mysterious person carries a singular receptacle wrought from the bark of trees, pauses before a cluster of perennials, bows submissively before them, then utters an exultant triumph and disappears like magic when seen. His physical features are described as being erect as a pole and wisps of gray hair covered his head. His trousers are blue jeans and fringed below the knees, his coat is yellow and sleeveless.[17]

◆

A "WILD MAN OF THE WOODS" MAY HAVE MURDERED WOMAN

This Is the Conjecture in Scranton, Where the Body of Mrs. McDonnell Was Found Jammed Into Crevice in Rocks

SCRANTON, Pa., Dec. 25 — The theory that the brutal murder of Mrs. Celia McDonnell, of Dunmore, was accomplished by some maniac is growing in favor with the police. Last fall the boulevard in the immediate region of the speedway where Mrs. McDonnell's body was found, was the scene of a number of exciting adventures by small pedestrian parties with a "wild man of the woods." A strange-looking being, with shaggy hair, long nails, and wearing only a ragged clout, was reported to have chased a boy and two young women who were strolling home from Lake Scranton, in the early evening.

Little attention was paid to the matter until others reported having encountered a similar experience, and then the police of Scranton and Dunmore investigated. They found the reports true, but could get no trace of the wild man. Chief Robling was then of the opinion that it was some demented man who had escaped from the custody of his family and became violent from the hardships of living in the mountain.

Extensive inquiry was made, with a view of proving this theory, but nothing came of it. Chief Robling now thinks it not at all improbable that this wild man has wandered back to the region of the speedway again, and that it was he who perpetrated the fiendish crime.

The inquest will be held tomorrow night, but unless something new is discovered tomorrow there will be little or no evidence at hand to show any light either on the murderer or the motive for the crime.[18]

WILD MAN WHO LOOKS LIKE GORILLA MADE CRAZY BY JOHNSTOWN FLOOD

HOLLIDAYSBURG, Pa., Feb. 27 — Blair county has a wild man. He was made crazy by the Johnstown flood, and has been living ever since in the woods and amid rocks. Only recently he came into public notice at Blue Knob, a county hamlet, located among the peaks of the Alleghenies.

In accordance with the theory of evolution this strange creature, who has forgotten even his own name, looks, by this time, very much like a wild animal or gorilla. Farmers and their families along the mountain side are frequently terrified by his unexpected appearances before them in unfrequented places.[19]

WEIRD NIGHT SOUNDS

Footsteps and Rappings at Odd Hours.

IS THE HOUSE HAUNTED?

A West Side Family Disturbed By Uncanny Manifestations.

People living in a certain large West Side house have been greatly annoyed of late by the queer happenings at the most unexpected times and in the most inexplicable manner.

The family is not anxious for publicity and it was only the merest chance that a reporter of this paper gained the information that a veritable haunted house existed in Greenville.

It will be remembered that last summer a wild man was said to be at large on the West Side, he having frightened many people and when efforts were made to catch him he would mysteriously disappear. Whether or not that strange character has anything to do with the present manifestations has not been determined, but that some unknown character or object is disturbing the peace and nerves of the people living in the house, is certain.

To the man of the most steady nerves the sound of footsteps in a portion of the house he knows to be unoccupied will cause more or less of a creepy sensation and that is one of the things which is of common occurrence in the house to which we refer.

The sound of some one walking across the up stairs floor at any hour of the day or night is not unusual but the effort to find any person there has been unsuccessful.

At other times, rappings, as if made by some one wishing to call attention, are heard but from what they emanate has not been learned. Sighs and faint moanings, the opening and closing of doors, are thrown in by way of variety. Altogether it is very trying to those who have to stay and listen to these weird and uncanny demonstrations.

The family has tried to solve the mystery and hoped to be left undisturbed, but in spite of all they can do in the way of locking doors, fastening windows and securing everything that might cause queer sounds by the action of the wind, the manifestations continue and the family will not live long in the present quarters should there not be an abatement of the nerve racking, spooky sounds.[20]

READING. — Special Detective John Smith, of the Mt. Penn Gravity Railway, and a posse of citizens have been unsuccessfully searching Mt. Penn for a wild man who created considerable excitement last fall, and who was seen again Thursday night. It is believed that he is an escaped lunatic from some asylum, and that he lived on the mountain all winter, sleeping in the basement of one of the houses, which are deserted in the cold months. When approached the wild man gives a yell, butts his head against a tree and then takes to his heels. His clothing is in tatters.[21]

———◆———

— An explorer has returned from the wilds of Africa and claims to have discovered an ape-man. Well, some of those things can be found much nearer home.[22]

———◆———

A wild man is said to be running at large in the townships of West Mead and Randolph, east of the city. He has been seen by several persons, but always manages to run away. According to report he wears no clothes, has long, disheveled hair and his general appearance is that of an animal more than a human being.[23]

———◆———

WILD BEAST OR WILD MAN?

Curious Creature Which Has Alarmed the Vicinity of Harmonsburg, This County.

A Harmonsburg special to the *Meadville Star* describes a strange wild animal recently seen in that vicinity which has awakened much curiosity and not a little alarm. It is yellow and brown in color, with heavy shoulders and a large head. The beast when set upon by dogs fights ferociously. Parties have been organized to hunt down the animal, which is said to answer the description of one which recently made its escape from captivity in Cleveland. *The Herald* recently made reference to a report that a "wild man" was running loose in the same vicinity, and presumably the two stories have one and the same origin.[24]

ATTACKED BY A GORILLA

Colored Man Has Encounter With Escaped Beast

BRIDGEVILLE, Nov. 20 — Frank Biles, colored, was nearly killed last night by a gorilla near Bethel camp ground, eight miles from here. It is said the gorilla escaped from a circus menagerie at Seaford.

Biles was riding a wheel to Cannon's when he was attacked. It threw him from the wheel and dealt him a heavy blow with its fist. The man in some manner pulled his revolver and shot twice, making his escape to Cannon's. Upon reaching Cannon's he was unable to speak for some time. A crowd gathered about the man, his clothing was in shreds and he had an ugly wound over the ear.

A posse of about fifty men was formed to capture the animal.[25]

Wild Man at Hunter's Station

While Ben Machamer and several other hunters from Shamokin were roaming the woods near Hunter's Station yesterday they came upon a cave that is inhabited by a hermit. The man appears to be demented and it is thought that he is the man who escaped from authorities in the Lower Mahanoy Valley last May. In his cave were some half decayed vegetables and part of a pig. The farmers thereabouts think they have found the author of the depredations on their storehouses during the last summer.[26]

The wild man who molested the peace of mind of College avenue above the bridge some years ago is said to be on hand again.[27]

The wild man still goeth about College avenue, seeking whom he may devour, nothwithstanding Allie Burns' furious onslaught with a rapid-fire revolver.[28]

Wild Man in Erie County.

CORRY, PA., June 12 — A wild man is exciting the neighborhood of Carre Hill, near here. When the male members of the family are away the man appears, frightening the woman away and stealing food. Children fear to go on the roads alone.[29]

PIKE COUNTY'S WILD WOMAN

Twice Seen Lately by Hunters in Kettle Creek Region.

IS AS FLEET AS A DEER

Her Appearance Haggard and at Sight of Man She Darts Away in the Forest With the Shriek of a Wild Animal.

GALETON, Pa., July 5 — Twice with in the past two weeks have Pike county men coming out of the Kettle creek region reported seeing a wild woman in the hemlock forest there. Philip Crippen and George DeHass both saw her while on a trout-fishing expedition below Aleona. DeHass had his attention attracted by the breaking of a limb but a few yards from him in the bushes, and turning saw what he first believed was a bear. He whipped out his navy pistol and was about to shoot when he saw that the fleeing object was not a bear, but a half-dressed woman, whose long black hair fell in an unkempt mass over her shoulders.

DeHass, frightened at how near he had come to murdering a human being, was so much overcome that he made no attempt to pursue the creature, who went at a breakneck pace into the thicket of laurel which lined the ravine. Subsequent examination showed that she had been lying in a thicket of maples, from which she darted when awakened, or aroused, by the sound of DeHass clambering over the rocks. The woman had placed several pieces of hemlock bark across two poles, and beneath this flimsy shelter she had evidently lain for some time. The few seconds' glimpse that DeHass got proved her to be without hat or shawl, and the lining of her dress showed in places where the outer fabric had been torn in shreds.

Crippen, the companion of DeHass, who was down stream a

rod or two, had a decided scare over the maniac-looking creature, who, before seeing him, had tried to ford the creek so as to get into deeper and darker woods on the other side. Crippen was wading the stream, when, above the sound made by the rushing water, his ear caught the piercing scream of a woman. He turned and saw the haggard face of a female glancing at him from between some alder bushes.

LIKE A HUNTED HARE

He was hardly twenty feet from her and in the instant that the mad creature halted he had an excellent opportunity to observe her features. He thinks she could have been no more than 35 years of age, and despite her frightened, hunted look he saw traces of beauty in her face. Her eyes, like her hair, were dark and shone like those of a hunted hare. When she started away she bent low and scooted through the brushes and briers with the alacity of a girl in her teens.

Several theories are advance in explanation of the woman's presence there. It is reported from Tioga county that an insane woman who was about to be taken to the Warren Asylum escaped from her home the night set for her departure for the asylum. The timbered section of the county is such between Marsh creek and the Kettle creek region that she could easily have stolen across without detection, though the journey would have been a long and rough one. Then, too, is said the wife of a Hungarian laborer, living in the vicinity of Hyner, Clinton county, going insane over the death of her baby, fled from the home because she feared that somebody pursued her to take her life, too.

SEEN ONCE AGAIN

A woodsman named Stauffer saw the wild woman last. Stauffer was traveling from a lumber camp near county line to a job near New Bergen. It was in the dusk of the evening, and he had stopped to eat a sandwich at a spring along the pike. It was at a place where a trough had been erected for horses and where teamsters driving that way are in the habit of stopping to feed and water their horses. Half-eaten ears of corn were scattered over the ground. Suddenly he heard the unmistakable sound of a human cough, and saw a woman stooping over gathering the ears of corn, now and then stopping long enough to munch a mouthful of the grains off a cob, and then thrust the latter, with the others, in her bosom. She was such a frightful looking creature that Stauffer, big, lusty fellow that he is, was half afraid to speak to her. It was while he stood hesitating that the wild woman caught sight of him; then, like a frightened rabbit, she ran into the woods after giving utterance to a shriek that Stauffer says he heard but once before, and that was in a madhouse when an attendant tried to force a woman maniac into her cell. Stauffer made no effort to follow her, electing rather to let the eerie spot as far behind him as possible before dark.[30]

———◆———

GIRARDVILLE. — While searching for his lost cow on the mountain near Frog Hollow, Joseph Anderson was yesterday given an unpleasant surprise by an unclothed wild man, about six foot in height, emerging from behind a tree. Anderson, becoming greatly unnerved, started on a wild run homeward. The man, however, unmindful of his presence, continued on his wild tramp through the street. He is thought to be an escaped lunatic from the asylum, as he was seen two weeks ago near Ringtown.[31]

———◆———

TAMAQUA has a "wild man!" Before the weird looking individual reached the woods without being captured, half the populace was at his heels. The strange individual emerged from the cellar of a church. His head was covered with a mass of matted hair reaching to the shoulders, while his face was covered with a shaggy beard. The remnants of a suit of clothes hung in tatters from his body, while his feet were wrapped in bags, held in place with rope and twine. Everything indicated that he had lived in the mountains for a long time, and that he had been driven to the town by hunger. Tall and gaunt, he covered the distance through the town with such fleetness that he resembled an animal evading capture.[32]

———◆———

There is another wild man roaming around Fairmont and parties say it is of giant stature, wild and dangerous looking.[33]

———◆———

WHOOP! WILD MAN
LOOKS WILD ENOUGH
TO EAT 'EM ALIVE

MOUNT JOY, Pa., Nov. 15 — Farmers living about Hill Church, north of here, are somewhat disturbed over the antics of a supposed wild man.

According to persons who have seen him, the wild man carries a bowl, made of tree bark, and seems to have neglected to visit a barber for several years.

Several times he has been observed bowing politely to a clump of trees, a performance which he concludes each time with a terrible whoop, and then quickly vanishes.[34]

———◆———

WILD MAN IN CEMETERY.

Officers Gave Chase to Nude Negro in Highwood Cemetery.

An insane negro, stark naked and his black form standing in sharp contrast with the tombstones, is the cause of terror to visitors to the Highwood Cemetery, Allegheny. A fusillade of shots fired at the wild man yesterday afternoon in the cemetery by Police Lieutenant John Bolland and several policemen and a chase which lasted for half an hour failed to bring about his capture.

Superintendent John Feguson, of the cemetery, caught sight of the burly negro running wildly through Section No. 2 and reported the matter at once to the police. Lieutenant Bolland and a squad of policemen went to the cemetery and began a search. About 4 o'clock they found the object of their search in a thick clump of trees. The negro started in the direction of Marshall's woods and the officers opened fire, but the distance was too great for any of the bullets to take effect. Nothing more was seen of him yesterday. Superintendent Ferguson said that he has seen him at different times for the past several weeks. How he subsists in the cemetery is not known. He is described as weighing about 160 pounds and being about 30 years old.[35]

———◆———

HAYS BOROUGH CITIZENS ARE ON "WILD MAN" HUNT

Searching parties were scouring the woods in the neighborhood of Hays borough last night for a "wild man." Early in the afternoon Alma, aged 9, and Edna, aged 11, daughters of John Jackson of Hays borough, were playing in their woods near their home when a powerful negro, entirely nude, is reported to have burst out upon them from the underbrush emitting frightful yells as he made his way toward them. The children ran to their home screaming with fright, George Jackson, their uncle, attracted by the screams of the children and the frantic cries of the negro, who turned back into the woods. The "wild man" made his escape.[36]

◆

NUDE WILD MAN SPREADS TERROR IN THE SUBURBS

Germantown and Chestnut Hill Residents Alarmed by a Supposed Maniac

Was Seen in Private Grounds on Sunday Morning, and Chased by Fireman, But Escaped

The police of Germantown and Chestnut Hill stations are endeavoring to capture a man whom they believe to be a dangerous maniac and who has terrorized the residents of the suburb for two weeks by roaming about wooded sections in a nude state uttering blood-curdling yells.

He is known as the "wild man of the woods," and although he has been pursued a number of times he evades his pursuers by seeking the shelter of the woods, where all trace of him is lost. It is thought that the man is living in one of the many caves along part of the Wissahickon Creek little frequented, and Park guards are making a systematic search to locate his hiding place.

Seen Sunday Morning

The wild man's latest appearance was on Sunday, when he was discovered on the grounds of Mrs. J. B. Stevenson's residence, at Greene street and Walnut lane, at an early hour. The same morning he was pursued by Joseph Naegle, a fireman of Engine Company 19.

The man only makes his appearance in the early morning and late at night. He has been seen by the scores of people lurking in the woods about the beautiful Lincoln drive.

Byways bordering on the park are little frequented by people, who fear the man may attack them.[37]

◆

A wild man is reported roaming at large in the section of country around Taylorstown.[38]

◆

Think It Was a Wild Man.

CONNELLSVILLE, Pa., Aug. 2 — Deputy Coroner J. E. Sims and a party of searchers spent all yesterday afternoon searching for the body of a man reported to have been seen lying on a ledge in the vicinity of Little Rock. Three children reported seeing the body. They lead the coroner to the place, but no trace of the man could be found. The officers believe the man, who was naked, is a wild man, who had been taking a nap on the rocks.[39]

◆

BOYS ON AN EXPLORING TRIP SEE WILD MAN AND FLEE FOR THEIR LIVES

Supposed Runaway from Insane Asylum Gives Youngsters the Scare of Their Lives When They Encounter Him After Following His Tracks.

"Look — look, boys — it's a wild man!" yelled Seldyn Taylor to his boy companions, as he stood open-mouthed staring at a sight that made his blood run cold. The boys were near Lowrys run, north of Avalon, at 5 o'clock yesterday afternoon.

Young Taylor's comrades turned and looked where he pointed. Crouched as if to spring, was a big, black-bearded, ghoul-faced thing, resembling half-man and half-gorilla glaring at the boys on the ridge above him.

Then he straightened up, put both great claw-like hands up

as if to clutch the boys, and uttered a hoarse animal growl which set the boys off on the race of their lives. They never looked back to view again that fearful sight.

The boys, among them Andy Ball, son of a farmer who lives near Ben Avon; Seldyn Taylor, 14-year old son of Samuel Taylor, a farmer; Louis Jackman, and Fred Brochouner, a dairy woman's son of Kilbuck township, were on an exploring expedition. They found tracks in the sand and followed the direction of the footprints until they came upon a smoldering fire with three sticks set up and wired together. All around were scattered fowl's feathers and garbage from garden vegetables. The curiosity of the boys was stimulated by these discoveries, and eagerly they searched the vicinity.

While doing this young Taylor screamed: "Look, boys — it's a wild man!" and he told the truth. The man was barefooted and naked to the waist, only a worn frayed pair of trousers hiding his lower limbs. The boys had heard rumors for the last week of a strange man in the neighborhood and this had excited their curiosity, resulting in the hunting expedition.

The man's legs were bare to the knees, the bushes and weeds and thorns having torn the trouser legs away until they hung in rags. His face was thin and gaunt, as if he suffered from starvation.

Farmers of Killbuck township have been missing chickens and other fowls regularly, and much garden truck has been mysteriously disappearing. The only explanation that can be given is that the wild man is an escaped inmate of the insane asylum at Dixmont, who, about six weeks ago, broke away from the guards and escaped toward Ben Avon, where all trace of him was lost.[40]

———◆———

They have found a wild man near Ben Avon, with long hair, like a gorilla. About the only missing party recalled is the author of tracts on Canadian steel rail prices.[41]

———◆———

WILD MAN

Fought the Captors and Made His Escape After One Had Been Badly Bitten

PITTSBURGH, Pa., July 21 — The wild man, supposed to be an escaped patient from

Dixmont, who has been terrorizing the boroughs of Ben Avon, Avalon, and Elmsworth, was caught by a party of Ben Avon citizens, but made his escape later.

J.S. Wagoner, Charles and Robert Crawford, and John Trust, while returning home, were accosted by a man with long hair all over his body and who had the appearance of a full grown gorilla.

Mr. Wagoner, as well as Charles Crawford, immediately gave battle, and with the assistance of Robert Crawford succeeded in getting the supposed wild man down on the ground. Mr. Trust took his handkerchief and bound the wild man's wrists behind his back, but when they allowed him to rise the lunatic began kicking and biting in such a manner that all parties concerned were only too glad to let him go. Straining his wrists, he managed to get his hands free, and he ran to a nearby tree and went up with the agility of a cat.

Wagoner and Trust were left to watch while the Crawford brothers went home and secured lanterns and additional help, but when they returned they could find no signs of Wagoner and Trust or the supposed wild man. They searched the locality and found no signs of either. Then they started home and when near Crawford's farm caught up with the watchers, who gave an exciting account of their experiences, stating that the wild man came down the tree and gave them a fierce battle, in which Wagoner was badly bitten and scratched and his clothing badly torn.[42]

---◆---

SAY THEY SAW A GORILLA.

Wilkes-Barre Mountain May Have New Species if Animal.

Greatly excited were the residents of Georgetown, Laurel Run and along the Wilkes-Barre mountains yesterday, when a big, ugly gorilla made its appearance and frightened a score of people.

Many were of the opinion that it was a bear, but others who came in contact with the brute, state positively that it is not, but a gorilla of the most pronounced type. Its howls can be heard distinctly at night and it prowls about in the daytime, and while several men, as well as two young women, had a run for their lives, they did not care to make a statement, saying that they would be ridiculed.

Two young women, who would not disclose their names,

were the first to make known the fact that a wild beast was roaming the woods. They were on their way home from Laurel Run and looking behind saw what they thought a gorilla striding across the roadway. The young women took to their heels and arrived at their respective homes unharmed, though breathless and badly frightened. The story of their experience soon became known and in less time than it takes to tell it, there were all kinds of rumors afloat. A foreigner stated that he had the same kind of an experience.

Then it was said that James Clarke, who resides along the Wilkes-Barre mountain, also saw the animal.[43]

◆

MORTON'S GORILLA STIRS 'EM.

Folks Who Don't Drink, Like Those Who Do, See Him.

CHESTER, Pa., Oct. 31 — The negroes residing in and about Morton and Springfield are still being terrorized by the monstrosity, which, it is said, resembles a gorilla, and which has been roaming about with the speed of a deer. Many persons who are compelled to travel by the lonely place at night have armed themselves with revolvers.

Charles Dotts, a white farmer, declares that he saw the strange beast and that he shot it several times but the bullets did not appear to have any effect except that the animal snorted, tore up several small trees and then scampered off.

Harry Batty, a butcher, attributes his loss of fifty chickens on Monday night to the strange animal, which ate the entrails of the fowls and left the carcasses on the ground.

Daniel Norris is willing to make affidavit that he has frequently seen the freak and that the last time he saw the animal it was enjoying a bath in Whiskey Run, a small stream in Morton.

While driving to his home in Springfield last evening William Holliday says he saw a strange object some distance ahead of him, and that when he reached the top of the hill, on Woodland avenue, the animal, which looked like a gorilla, disappeared in a clump of bushes.

Others who declare they saw the mysterious animal are H. J. Mason, Frank Toland, Elwood Powell, and Joseph Johnson.

Many of the negroes are going around armed to the teeth, in readiness to meet the strange wonder.[44]

NEGROES SCARED BY GORILLA LIKE GHOST

PHILADELPHIA, Nov. 9 — Negro residents of Springfield township and Morton are tremendously agitated over a wild and uncanny thing resembling a gorilla, which, they say, is wandering about the neighborhood at night.

It walks on its hind legs, and makes its appearance about dusk. Apparently it manifests itself only to persons of African descent, for none of the white citizens have seen it as yet.

One negro says it growled at him a few nights ago, and that growl was sufficient inducement to him to run all the way home.

Another asserts that he shot the beast, but that the bullet bounded off as though it had struck a chunk of armor plate.[45]

Strange Beast in Pennsylvania.

Residents of Georgetown and Laurel Run, on the mountain near here, have been frightened by some strange animal during the last few days, which they say has appeared from the brush along the mountain road between the two places. Opinions as to what it is differ.

Some say it is an enormous ape and others that it is a bear which has wandered down from the Bear creek district, where they are plentiful. Those who have seen it have not waited to make any investigation, but have fled as fast as they could.[46]

APE-LIKE ANIMAL SCARES PEOPLE IN DELAWARE COUNTY

Trap Set for It Pulled Up by Roots and Wires and Chains Snapped

DARBY, Pa., Nov. 24 — All Delaware county is exercised over the antics of a strange, gorilla-like animal, which has been frightening belated pedestrians almost out of their wits in widely separated parts of the county within the last two weeks. One night it was seen near Chester, another night it was seen prowling near Media, and again it was seen running along the roads on all fours in Morton.

Runs Like Race Horse

Walking sometimes upright like a man, or else running along at race horse speed on all fours, with a peculiar leaping stride, and covered with a heavy coat of hair, the animal is differently described by those who see it. The negroes have become terrorized, and in many sections of the county cannot be induced to pass certain localities after dark where the animal has been seen. Others have stocked themselves with all manner of weapons to put an end to the freak and still have fled.

Some are of the opinion that it is an escaped ape from the Zoo, which is strengthened by the fact that a representative from the Zoological Gardens was making inquiries in Springfield township a few days ago concerning it. Traps have been set for it, only to be pulled up by the roots and the heavy wires and chains snapped like sugar-twine.

Bear Traps Too Weak

Frank Carr, of Springfield, aided by several of his neighbors, last Tuesday week got out two heavy steel bear traps, baited and set them. The strange animal had been seen lurking in the woods nearby at nights, and it was determined to capture it. The traps were set in an enclosure in the back of Mr. Carr's house, but the next morning both were sprung, the bait eaten off, and a section of heavy telegraph wire, with which they were fastened to a big oak tree, was snapped like a thread. The ground was clawed up as if newly furrowed, and the traps were found several rods away, as if carried that distance before the animal released itself. It was reported last Sunday night as having been seen in Media, on Washington street, near the residence of United States Marshal John B. Robinson, but it disappeared in the darkness.[47]

---------◆---------

FREAK CAUSES FEAR IN DELAWARE COUNTY

Strange Creature Startles Men in Chester Saloon, Then Vanishes — Traps Set, But Game Escapes

CHESTER, Nov. 25 — The Delaware county freak, that is said to be half man and half baboon, has reached this city. It made its debut in Chester society Friday night. As in most of the appearances of this creature the apparition was visible only from the door of a hotel.

Elwood Reed, who lives at Sixth and Central avenue, was in Edward Fry's saloon, one square from his home, during the night, and as he opened the door to leave he was confronted by what he says looked like a gorilla. It had claw-like hands and a head with a low, backward sloped forehead, but the legs were those of a man, for the creature wore shoes and pantaloons very much like those sold in the second-hand stores on Third street, but the form in front of him was hatless.

Speaking of the affair, Reed says: "I was never so frightened in all my life. I stood and gasped, then the thing grinned at me and ran across the street. Then I bolted from the room and raced down the street to my home, dashed in and got my gun."

Mr. Richardson, the bartender, also saw the freak and says that all of the men in the barroom turned ashen pale. Later it was learned that those frightened men were negroes, each of whom had, in the vernacular of the saloon, been "hitting them" during the evening.

On the way home one of the men saw the freak in the woods near the hotel washing a cabbage head in Lamokin run. Thus far Chester's policemen have not come up with a thing, whose only mission in this city is to keep frightened children indoors at night and incidentally make some men stay away from saloons.

Negroes in all parts of the county have been put in a state of terror by the stories of the strange animal, which always runs when approached. Horntown, Media Park, and other negro settlements quake when the subject is mentioned, and few black men venture out at night.

Efforts to trap the animal have been made by white men. Frank Carr, of Springfield, set two large bear traps, as the creature was said to be lurking in the woods, but the next morning the traps were found to have been sprung and the bait eaten away.

While opinion inclines in some quarters to the belief that an escaped ape is giving all this uneasiness, the accepted belief is that a half-witted wandering negro is the freak.[48]

◆

Down in Chester county where State Treasurer Berry makes bricks a new species of spook or ghost has appeared which seems to have originated in the fancy of some one who wanted to scare chicken thieves. It has the face of a man and the body of a gorilla and blows fire from its mouth. Several citizens more or less reputable say they saw the monster. A man who could see anything like that in Chester county must have been using vitascope whisky where, with every three drinks, one sees moving pictures.[49]

DARBY'S GORILLA ESCAPES POLICEMEN

Gives Them Slip in Darkness, After Keeping Ahead for Nearly an Hour

DARBY, Pa., Nov. 27 — The mysterious gorilla-like animal, which is said to have been seen in various parts of the county the past two weeks, showed up in the outskirts of Darby early this morning. That it is some strange freak of nature is not the least in doubt, according to Policemen Smith and Clark, who suddenly came upon the ape-like thing.

When they first saw it, it had the aspect of a big, wooly Newfoundland dog. He was coming down the middle of the road, but when it saw them it stopped and, standing upright, turned around and dashed away on all fours. They gave chase, but were unable to lessen the distance.

The "thing" seemed unusually intelligent, and kept just enough distance between it and its pursuers. They chased it around the outskirts of the borough nearly an hour before it gave them the slip and disappeared in the darkness.

Both policemen are full of nerve, but at no time could they get within shooting distance of it.

Theresa Quinn, the 14-year old daughter of Policeman Quinn, ran into the house yesterday badly frightened, saying that she had seen a man with a monkey head, but nothing was thought of the affair at the time. Several others have seen it, and the residents are becoming exercised over it.[50]

CLOSE ON "ITS" TRAIL

Delaware County Bogey Man Believed to Be Predatory Polander

CHESTER, Nov. 27 — The residents of Clifton Heights and vicinity believe that they have discovered the identity of the half-man and half-gorilla that has been prowling about Delaware county. Last evening a Polander, of Oak Hill, near Clifton Heights, stopped two children who were on an errand to the store and stole what little money they had in their possession.

The father of the children hastened to the spot where the robbery occurred, and he saw the foreigner lurking about waiting for other victims. The Polander, whose face is covered with a thick beard, dashed toward Kellyville. This man is said to be the one who has been robbing school children of their pennies and taking advantage of intoxicated men. He generally lurked between Kent's Mills and St. Charles Catholic church, in Kellyville.

The authorities of Clifton Heights have ascertained the identity of the Polander who has been skulking about the borough and vicinity, and it is expected that his arrest will follow shortly.[51]

GORILLA SEEN AGAIN

DARBY, Pa., Nov. 28 — Apparently emboldened by the excited attitude of the people towards it, the gorilla-like being which, according to reports, has been causing all kinds of excitements in various parts of Delaware county the past two weeks, turned up again, so it is asserted, in several places early this morning, long enough in one to be shot at three times by a policeman, near Clifton Heights.

"Spot" Evans, a colored man, who lives on Hook road, on the outskirts of Sharon Hill, says that when on his way home from Darby early this morning, and half a mile up Chester pike, he heard something running after him. He turned and saw a big wooly object, which followed him to his home. Evans was so frightened that he got his gun, but by the time he reached the second-story to shoot it from the window it had slunk away in the woods.

Whatever the thing is, real or imagined, it has the people thoroughly aroused, and the negroes are terrified.[52]

Negro Gorilla Skin an Ogre.

The alleged monstrosity, supposed to be half man half gorilla, which has been frightening people the past week in Delaware county, made its appearance in Upland the other night.

Several young men of Upland were passing the Crozer Theological Seminary when they saw the freak, chased it, and one of the pursuers declares that it was a negro attired in the skin of a gorilla.

The freak also invaded the negro precinct in the western section of Chester late Tuesday night and greatly frightened the inhabitants.

The police have been instructed to arrest the thing, whatever it is, on sight.⁵³

DARBY'S "GORILLA" PROVES TO BE A DOG

Is "Arrested" by a Policeman and Viewed by Many Citizens.

DARBY, Pa., Nov. 30 — The "arrest" of a big brown-haired dog with an enormous head and an exceptionally long body last night by Policeman Clark, is believed to have solved Delaware county's mysterious gorilla-like bugaboo, which has been terrorizing belated pedestrians.

Clark came across the animal on Main street, and, drawing his gun, he made his way cautiously toward it, step by step. When he came within a few yards it turned and ran, with a peculiar leaping motion and its long matted hair, which flew out, gave it an aspect like that of the much-talked-of "gorilla."

After a chase of a square in the darkness Clarke threw his arms around the fleeing mystery, threatening to shoot it if it showed fight and found that it was a dog.

Thinking that its presence would explain the gorilla-man mystery, he took it to the station house and locked it up. Hundreds of people journeyed to the jail and had a look at the animal, although many negroes would not venture near it, fearing that it might break out.⁵⁴

"GORILLA" DEMON ONLY CRAZY NEGRO

Wearing Bear's Skin and Hair Daubed With Phosphorus He Was a Terror

SHARON HILL, Dec. 2 — The mystery of Delaware county's strange ape-like creature, that for the past fortnight has been prowling from village to village, terrorizing scores of men, women, and children, has been solved, according to Charles Wagner, a detective, of Philadelphia.

From the investigation which he and another operator carried on several nights ago in the vicinity of Darby, he learned that the wild-eyed demon was none other than a crazed negro, who makes his home in a shanty on the outskirts of this town.

With a rug of bearskin thrown over his body and his hair daubed with phosphorous, the negro, the sleuth asserts, stalked about the county roads, and on several occasions ventured to secret himself at an extremity of town.

Jumping and yelling as pedestrians passed, the demented man caused much excitement. Stories circulated about him increased the fear of the farmers and soon it was gossiped around that a "gorilla" was at large.

Detective Wagner has placed the man under surveillance. Means will be taken at once to have him removed to some institution.[55]

------♦------

Strange Animal Is Seen.

Wilkes-Barre, Pa. — Several parties living near the Wilkes-Barre mountain report that within the last few days they have seen a strange animal in the woods resembling a gorilla. At first it was thought it might be a bear but two hunters who saw the strange creature the other day claim it climbs trees like a monkey and goes into hiding upon the approach of men.[56]

------♦------

STRANGE MONSTER SCARES CITIZENS

WEIRD BABOON-LIKE CREATURE SEEN NEAR DARBY, PA.

MAY BE PRACTICAL JOKE

Belated Wayfarer of Delaware County Frightened by Mysterious Thing and Many Residents Are Arming Themselves.

Darby, Pa. — All Delaware county is stirred up over the supposed antics of an alleged wild animal which is asserted to look like a gorilla and to have frightened belated wayfarers almost out of their wits in various parts of the county. While it is believed by most persons that the whole thing is a practical joke on the part of some one who is literally making a monkey out of himself, still many of the more timid class are thoroughly alarmed and fully believe all the tales that are told about the mysterious creature.

Those professing to have seen the wonderful animal, assert that it sometimes goes upright like a man and then dashes along on all fours with marvelous speed, maintaining a queer galloping gait. They furthermore feel certain that it has a coat of dark hair, but that is not considered remarkable, as the weather is cool. Their stories of how they almost encountered the strange beast have been so thrilling that many of the negroes in the county cannot be induced to pass the spots where it is said to have been seen. Others have purchased pistols and go about armed, fully resolved to sell their lives dearly should they encounter the mythical monster in any of its hypothetical haunts.

Others take the thing seriously without being unduly alarmed and they try to explain the matter. That it is an ape escaped from some zoological collection is the most commonly accepted theory. This was strengthened by a rumor that the authorities of the Zoological Gardens of Philadelphia were out looking for a lost Simian in Delaware county. But a telephone message to the zoo exploded the story. All the Philadelphia monkeys are safe in their cages. Their keeper respectfully suggested that the animal down in Darby is probably a monkey of native Delaware county stock.

Nevertheless, several persons in Springfield township are so convinced that there is a strange animal prowling about that they have set traps for it. Frank Carr is one of them, and he set a number of traps in an enclosure in the rear of his house near some woods where the creature was reported to have been seen. It is now stated that the traps were found broken, the bait devoured and all evidence on hand of a struggle made by some animal.

The practical joker who is working the scare, if such is the case, has succeeded to an extent which may work his own harm. For there are a number of Delaware county citizens who, while not getting in hysterics about the matter, have quietly placed big guns in their hip pockets and are waiting for a chance to pot anything that looks like a baboon.[58]

Chased By Wild Man.

Pittson. — A party of berry pickers from Yatesville borough went into the woods for huckleberries and returned home shortly afterward badly frightened. They avowed they had been chased by a wild man, dirty in appearance, scantily clad and with disheveled hair. He screamed at them in a wild manner. The men of the village organized a party and searched the woods, but have not yet made his capture.[59]

NOW IT'S A BABOON MYSTERY.

Strange Animal Was First Classed as a Kangaroo.

Pennsburg, Pa., Aug. 26. — It is now asserted that the strange wild animal which has been alarming rural districts west of here, and which was supposed to be a kangaroo, is a baboon. Farmers have seen or heard it over a territory of six miles in extent, between Gilbertsville and Perkiomen. On one occasion it was encountered in the old covered bridge across the Perkiomen at Merkley's Mill. No one has yet been able to approach near enough to give a satisfactory description of the animal. F. F. Huber, teller of the Farmer's National Bank, this borough, is organizing a party of men to go in search of the creature with dogs and guns.[60]

WILD MAN IN WOODS

Strange Creature Seen Roaming Half Naked in Vicinity of Farmington.

Farmington, Oct. 9 — A wild man is reported loose in the vicinity and has been seen several times roaming through the woods half dressed, without hat or coat, and at other times entirely nude. He has been seen in this condition, at one particular spot on the new road, standing a few feet back in the brush, holding an old shirt in his hand at arm's length. This man has not molested any one, and why he appears in this condition is hard to understand.[61]

LOOKS LIKE A SPECTRE, BUT NOISY AS WILD MAN

Whitehaired Apparition Scares Some Residents of Verona Almost Into Fits.

Who is the aged apparition with long white hair and beard, who, with groans and moans and blood-curdling screams raises the hair of residents of Verona in affright and with nimble feet almost gives them heart failure by going in swift pursuit? That is the question some of the citizens are puzzling over, particularly Elmer Bouchner, who fled in dismay on Tuesday night when the whitehaired terrifier chased him.

Bouchner started home late. In Parker street he saw the strange phantasm, at least he thought it was such until the awe inspiring figure let out a horrible shriek, got down on all fours and clawed the sidewalk and then launched itself at Bouchner. The latter's cries vied in volume with those of his pursuer for awhile, until he reached a sheltering doorway, where he cowered. The spectre passed on and Bouchner, peeping out trembling, beheld him disappear between two houses.

Nobody in the neighborhood knew anything the next day of the strange vision, for Bouchner investigated, but the residents of Parker street have been kept awake at night by the weird, inarticulate cries of the whitehaired old man. He is too noisy for a ghost and citizens are laying plans to capture him.[62]

A "wild man," dweller in a cave, is striking terror to the residents of Haydock Mountain, south of Quakertown.[63]

◆

WILD MAN FRIGHTENS BEN AVON RESIDENTS.

Strange-Looking Being Roams in Woods and Scares Women of Borough.

A "wild man" is reported to have been seen at Ben Avon, and many women of that suburb are afraid to venture out of doors. According to the description given the man is tall with long hair and wears little clothing.

Shortly after noon, yesterday, Mrs. William Becker and her daughter, Jessie, of Ridge avenue, were crossing Spruce Run bridge when the man suddenly appeared at the upper end. The women were frightened, and two young men chased the stranger up the densely wooded hollow, where he disappeared. It is said the man wore a black mask over the upper part of his face.

Other women of the borough are said to have been scared by the same creature recently. Some residents of Ben Avon are accustomed to getting off at Spruce Run bridge to save the extra fare, but now many are afraid to do this.[64]

◆

Wild Man Wears Red Shirt.

Garbed in tattered red shirt a supposed wild man has appeared in the woods along Wildwood avenue, partly in Penn township and partly in Verona. Early yesterday morning two boys saw him picking berries. He fled when discovered. Robert Hammond saw the man in a road in front of his home, jumping about and uttering gutteral sounds. The creature had a beard and shaggy gray hair. Hammond and Constable R. S. Davis, with several other men, made a futile search for the man.[65]

◆

WILD MAN SCARE AROUSED EAST BERLIN

Residents Barred Doors When They Heard That Weak Minded Man was in Town

East Berlin, Jan. 29. — A man large of frame, but not strong of mind, made his appearance on the streets here several days ago, and by his varied peculiarities, succeeded in bringing terror to the minds of many of the inhabitants. The people, with the aid of the school children, who also came into contact with the harmless imbecile, soon spread the news that a wild man was loose in town. The odd creature soon disappeared, but not before doors generally were barred and many strong men had sought safety in their attics.

Next day, however, a couple of newspaper canvassers came to town and by some caprice of fate both of them resembled the "wild man." Again the citizens took to their heels and again the doors were barred. It appeared evident that the "wild man" had only left to return with re-enforcement and that the town probably would be eaten up.

The canvassers made a few rounds but were nowhere received. Finally at a home on King street, a woman more bold than the rest, armed with a hatchet and a rolling pin, thrust her head from a second story window and inquired of the newspaper men, whether they were "wild" and "crazy." With this she closed the window.

The canvassers eyed each other for a few minutes, muttered a few things, not good-naturedly, and caught a waiting train for the next burg.[66]

———◆———

DISCOVERED A WILD MAN

Heber L. DeWitt Meets With a Startling Adventure

Heber L. Dewitt, of the south side, extra operator of the Pennsylvania railroad company, who just now is filling a position at Nanticoke, while exploring the West Nanticoke mountain Sunday afternoon discovered a veritable wild man.

It proved to be a most exciting adventure. For a long time rumors have been current that a wild man subsists on the bare and desolate summit of one of the remote ranges that rise west of the river. Mr. DeWitt, however, was not searching for the wild man, but, with several companions, was enjoying an afternoon stroll over the mountains.

The weather was of the right sort for an outing, and, allured by the romantic scenery they tramped further and further until they found themselves on Tillberry's knob, the furthest and most solitary of the several mountains that rise successively higher and higher.

They were in the act of ascending the last elevation that leads to the summit, when on looking upward, they beheld an apparition that startled them. Standing out in bold relief against the sky and calmly surveying them as they approached, was a gigantic human figure. He was clad in rags and tatters. He was bareheaded; his disheveled hair hung down upon his shoulders, while his shaggy beard, cut off square below his chin as if with some rude implement, imparted to him an appearance of wildness and savagery, the like of which one would never expect to behold on the mountains of Pennsylvania.

Heber and his companions, however, were determined to get all the facts and they resolutely approached the wild man. The latter stood his ground. As the men came up face to face with him he uttered a defiant grunt, while his deepest repulsive eyes flashed with anger.

An attempt was made to converse with him. He emitted a series of strange sounds, but there was no articulated speech.

Nearby was the man's abode — an arched structure, not more than six feet long by three high, composed of branches of trees, pieces of logs, mere slabs, and the like. It was the crudest kind of shelter, only large enough to cover the man lying at full length. At one end it was open; here it was protected by a log, over which the wild man was obliged to crawl in entering or leaving the hut — if so it might be called. The log at the entrance was worn smooth indicating that the strange and primitive abode had been the wild man's shelter for many years.

Many persons believe the lone hermit on Tillberry's knob is no other than a man who disappeared from Plymouth years ago, a foreigner who on being wronged by a citizen of the town declared that he would henceforth have nothing to do with his fellow man but retired to the solitude of the mountains to end his days.[67]

———————◆———————

MURDER RECALLED BY GHOSTLY TALES; HOME IS HAUNTED

Screams and Sight of Wild Man in Woods Revive Mystery.

MUNCY VALLEY IS EXCITED

EVERY ONE KEEPING DISTANCE FROM SECTION AFFECTED BY APPEARANCES.

LAPORTE, Pa., June 14 — Two recent reports having to do with the mysterious murder at Muncy Valley, on the night of December 20, 1905, of aged Sarah Whitmire renew public interest in one of the most atrocious killings in the history of Sullivan county, the object of which was presumed to be robbery, though there were other circumstances which pointed to a motive more terrible.

The little story-and-a-half house, directly alongside the Williamsport & North Branch Railroad, over which the traffic to Eaglesmere passes, in which the murder was committed, is said now to be haunted, while but a few weeks ago there came a dramatic story from the lumber woods of this county to the effect that a woodsman, finding himself at the verge of death from consumption, sent for the district preacher and made confession to him that he was the murderer of the old woman hermit, the crime having been committed with a stick of stove wood because the woman would not permit him to find shelter under her roof that night.

Described the Murder.

The woodsman, so the story ran, had been drinking at the town down the valley, and came to the lonely hut late in the evening. Seeing a light within he rapped for entrance, but when the old woman saw that it was a stranger she attempted to push the door shut; that he then forced his way into the room, and then she attacked him with a poker he grabbed a stick of wood and felled her to the floor: then, fearing she would scream he struck her again and again until she was quiet. The report of the woodsman's confession was so vague that but little creedence was placed in it, and it would have been passed away as another seven-day gossip if the rumor of a ghost being seen at the blood-smeared cabin had not started the little community down in the valley.

Footprints in the Snow.

Once last winter, when the

snow was deepest, a villager who stopped and went in from the road to the little house to peer into the windows, reported finding the tracks of a human being, barefoot, in the snow leading from the door into the woods a short distance away. The theory as to these tracks was that the murderer of the old woman, living somewhere in the wilds of Lower Sullivan and Northern Columbia county, had come through the storm to the scene of his crime, in accordance with the old belief that a murderer cannot stay away from the spot where he slew his victim.

The finding of tracks, too, recalled the fact that for several seasons hunters and fishermen have reported having seen a wild man in the territory lying off toward Jamison City.

Work of a Maniac.

When the body of the old woman was found stretched out on the floor of her kitchen, between the stove and the wood-box, her blood in pools upon the floor, and portions of her brains scattered against the boards of the partition, with a stick of stove-wood containing wisps of her grey hair on it, it was freely guessed that the slayer of old Mrs. Whitmire was a maniac. A woodsman was arrested between here and Eaglesmere, and after being in jail here for a few days,

was given a hearing and discharged, there being no evidence.

Now it is said that at a certain hour at night a strange light flickers through the little old house and that one night a few weeks ago a late passer-by heard a scream similar to that heard by a young preacher who was driving toward the house with his horse and buggy on a way from his meeting at Strawbridge on the night of the murder.[68]

◆

PEEPER IS A WOMAN

Whole Police Force Vainly Trying to Catch Feminine Athelete.

WASHINGTON, Pa., June 14 — Residents of two wards here are greatly excited over the antics of a mysterious "woman in black" who peeps in windows and appears at night in lawns and yards. Last night she appeared in several places and the entire police force and over 100 citizens tried to capture her.

The woman was almost cornered at a West Chestnut street house, where several men sprang out at her from a side door. She shook them off with apparent ease, vaulted a high fence and eluded capture. Many believe the masquerader is a man.[69]

———◆———

— A Westfield correspondent says: "There has been much discussion in regard to the wild man or animal which several people have seen on Mill creek, on the Broughton Hollow, and on the Jameson. Some think it may be a bear but those who have seen it report that, though it sometimes stands on all fours, it raises itself upon its hind legs to travel and gets itself along at a very good pace. It is reported to have chased one man and also at another time to have turned and ran away when it received a charge of bird shot in the face, from a gun in the hands of a boy. It is said to have more the resemblance of a wild man or gorilla than a bear. Some hunters have made a pretense at least of endeavoring to hunt it down, but without success."[70]

———◆———

WILD MAN IS SCARING MANY BERRY PICKERS

Huckleberry pickers from Beaver Meadow to Weatherly have reported that a wild man has chased them. The man is said to be scantily clad and yells and gesticulates when he rushes from his hiding places. His appearance has caused terror among the women and children, who for the most part comprise the army of berry pickers. It is believed that the man is either an escaped convict or lunatic. He was last seen along the line of the Lehigh Valley railroad.[71]

———◆———

Shot Cousin While Loading Gun.

Lancaster, Pa., Oct. 4 — Albert Kraft, aged thirteen years, was shot and almost instantly killed near Columbia by his cousin, Alfred Groom, seventeen years old. The elder lad had borrowed a revolver for the purpose of protecting himself from an alleged wild man and was loading it when the weapon was accidentally discharged.[72]

———◆———

Nude Wild Man Excites Mountville

Mountville, Pa., Oct. 9 — Much excitement has been aroused in this vicinity by the appearance of a wild man. Farmers are keeping watch at night, as they are afraid he may try to fire their barns. The last to see him was George McComsey, of Columbia, a track walker.

The man goes perfectly nude. His body is covered with hair. When any one approaches him he runs in the bushes and hides.

An attempt will be made to get him. He has been in this section for some time.[73]

MAN ROAMS NUDE IN WOODS

Columbia School Teacher Frightened by Supposed Lunatic

Columbia, Pa., Oct. 14 — Miss Hartman, a school teacher yesterday encountered the so-called wild man who has been frightening residents of this section for several weeks. As she was walking on a country road east of town she was startled by a piercing cry. A moment later an entirely nude man jumped in front of her, frantically waving his hands.

The woman ran and the man did not pursue her. The authorities will increase their efforts to capture the supposed lunatic.[74]

[1] *Connellsville Courier* (Connellsville, PA), February 2, 1900.

[2] *Harrisburg Telegraph* (Harrisburg, PA), March 1, 1900.

[3] *Pittsburgh Daily Post* (Pittsburgh, PA), March 16, 1900.

[4] *Harrisburg Telegraph* (Harrisburg, PA), June 12, 1900.

[5] *The Scranton Republican* (Scranton, PA), July 18, 1900.

[6] *The Scranton Tribune* (Scranton, PA), July 20, 1900.

[7] *The Scranton Republican* (Scranton, PA), July 20, 1900.

[8] *The Times* (Philadelphia, PA), July 21, 1900.

[9] *The Scranton Republican* (Scranton, PA), July 30, 1900.

[10] *The Record-Argus* (Greenville, PA), August 17, 1900.

[11] *The Record-Argus* (Greenville, PA), August 22, 1900.

[12] *The Record-Argus* (Greenville, PA), August 25, 1900.
An attempt at wild man humor from the newspaper.

[13] *The Philadelphia Inquirer* (Philadelphia, PA), October 16, 1900.

[14] *Lebanon Semi-Weekly News* (Lebanon, PA), November 11, 1900.
Unfortunately the copy of this article I turned up was very difficult to read - with some completely faded words. I was able to transcribe most of the article, however, and what a wondrous strange story it is! The following article seems to tell of the same individual.

[15] *Bradford Era* (Bradford, PA), November 23, 1900.

[16] *Juniata Sentinel and Republican* (Mifflintown, PA), November 28, 1900.

[17] *Lebanon Daily News* (Lebanon, PA), December 21, 1900.
Another tree-bower - or perhaps the same one, if he has given up his previously described black garb and exchanged his square package for a vessel of tree bark. Knee-length pants and a sleeveless coat seem mighty chilly for late December in Pennsylvania.

[18] *The Philadelphia Inquirer* (Philadelphia, PA), December 26, 1900.

[19] *The Philadelphia Inquirer* (Philadelphia, PA), February 28, 1901.
I'm not sure the writer quite understands the theory of evolution, however this notion - the idea that men would grow hair and begin to look like animals if they turned away from society - seems to be a prevailing theory expressed both directly and indirectly throughout these old wild man articles. Of course, humans do not grow any more hair just by turning away from society and becoming feral. I declare this "gorilla" a bigfoot!

[20] *The Record-Argus* (Greenville, PA), March 16, 1901.
I expect, at this stage in the book, the reader may be expecting me to say that the ghostly sounds mentioned in this article could be at the hands (or feet) of a bigfoot creature. While bigfoot are known to tap on windows, climb upon and walk on roofs, and create all manner of strange disturbances on the outside of peoples' homes, the instances of bigfoot creatures coming inside an occupied dwelling are exceedingly rare. The sounds in this article primarily, it seems, emanate from *within* the house. My reason for this article's inclusion is, as noted by the reporter, this haunting takes place in an area where a "wild man" was also seen. As I wrote in the introduction to this volume, I have found where you get bigfoot reports, you also get other strange phenomena. In this case ghosty or poltergeist-like activity.

During one of my appearances on *Where Did the Road Go?*, a radio program which explores fringe and paranormal topics, we were speaking about bigfoot. Fellow guest and author, Joshua Cutchin perceptively noted that many bigfoot behaviors seem to mirror poltergeist activity. Things being thrown (in the case of bigfoot, most often rocks), rapping, knocking, and loud bangs, disembodied screams and strange voices all find their way into both bigfoot experiences and hauntings. An excellent observation by Mr. Cutchin, and well worth noting here.

[21] *Wilkes-Barre Times* (Wilkes-Barre, PA), June 8, 1901.

[22] *The York Daily* (York, PA), June 21, 1901.

[23] *Titusville Herald* (Titusville, PA), October 10, 1901.

[24] *Titusville Herald* (Titusville, PA), October 17, 1901.

[25] *The Philadelphia Inquirer* (Philadelphia, PA), November 21, 1901.
No African gorilla, nor any other great ape save for humans, would survive very long in the wilds of Pennsylvania - and certainly not in late

November! Whatever attacked Frank Biles, it was not an African gorilla escaped from a circus.

[26] *The Daily News* (Mount Carmel, PA), November 29, 1901.

[27] *The Record-Argus* (Greenville, PA), May 6, 1902.

[28] *The Record-Argus* (Greenville, PA), May 16, 1902.

[29] *Pittsburgh Weekly Gazette* (Pittsburgh, PA), June 13, 1902.

[30] *The Times* (Philadelphia, PA), July 6, 1902.

[31] *Wilkes-Barre Times* (Wilkes-Barre, PA), August 26, 1902.

[32] *Lebanon Daily News* (Lebanon, PA), April 4, 1903.

[33] *The Weekly Courier* (Connellsville, PA), September 19, 1903.

[34] *The Philadelphia Inquirer* (Philadelphia, PA), November 16, 1903.
The bowing wild-man makes his return.

[35] *The Pittsburgh Press* (Pittsburgh, PA), June 28, 1904.
Bigfoot creatures have been noted, for some reason, to frequent cemeteries. Was this a case of misidentification? It seems extreme to fire on a man if roaming a cemetery nude was his only offense - though these were different times.

[36] *Pittsburgh Weekly Gazette* (Pittsburgh, PA), September 28, 1904.

[37] *The Philadelphia Inquirer* (Philadelphia, PA), October 4, 1904.

[38] *The Daily Notes* (Canonsburg, PA), June 22, 1905.

[39] *Pittsburgh Daily Post* (Pittsburgh, PA), August 3, 1905.

[40] *Pittsburgh Post-Gazette* (Pittsburgh, PA), July 11, 1906.

[41] *Pittsburgh Daily Post* (Pittsburgh, PA), July 20, 1906.

[42] *Advocate* (Newark, OH), July 21, 1906.
A fierce battle with what seems like a bigfoot creature from its appearance, aggressiveness, and tree-climbing.

[43] *Wilkes-Barre Times Leader, the Evening News* (Wilkes-Barre, PA), October 25, 1906.

[44] *The Scranton Republican* (Scranton, PA), November 1, 1906.
There have been many modern accounts of people shooting bigfoot creatures with no apparent effect. Likewise of the creatures tearing up trees, perhaps in warning or anger, as they fled from humans.

[45] *Oakland Tribune* (Oakland, CA), November 9, 1906.
Presumably reporting on the same story as the above article this shows, besides the blatant racism apparent in their story, the way details seem to change from paper to paper. The idea that only African Americans have seen the creature is directly contrasted in the *Scranton Republican* article.

[46] *Altoona Tribune* (Altoona, PA), November 14, 1906.

[47] *The Philadelphia Inquirer* (Philadelphia, PA), November 25, 1906.

[48] *The York Daily* (York, PA), November 26, 1906.

[49] *The Wilkes-Barre News* (Wilkes-Barre, PA), November 27, 1906.

[50] *The Philadelphia Inquirer* (Philadelphia, PA), November 28, 1906.
Here we have a creature seen, and chased, by *two* policemen. Bipedal-to-quadrupedal locomotion is noted, as well as the apparent intelligence of the creature.

[51] *The York Daily* (York, PA), November 28, 1906.
In this article the reporter takes an ugly sidestep from a racist explanation for the creatures to a xenophobic solution. This reasoning doesn't explain how or why other witnesses, including police officers, have described the creature as half-man and half-gorilla, nor does it mention the "foreigner" in question dropping down to all fours and running at the speed of a race horse. In short, this man who was robbing children, very likely had nothing to do with the "gorilla" reports coming from the area.

[52] *The Philadelphia Inquirer* (Philadelphia, PA), November 29, 1906.

[53] *The Central News* (Perkasie, PA), November 29, 1906.

[54] *Wilkes-Barre Times* (Wilkes-Barre, PA), November 30, 1906.
Yet another "explanation" for the creature - this time, a dog. This

seems to me like the police trying to calm the community by saying they had "solved" the mystery. This creature that could run as fast as a racehorse and previously outran two policemen for an hour is run down by Officer Clark in a short chase? All of the previous witnesses speaking of monkey-headed men, baboons, and gorillas had just misidentified a dog? A dog was responsible for taking the bait from bear traps, uprooting the traps, and breaking the heavy wires and chains that held the traps to an oak tree? This really must have been some canine! And yet, this dog is not the last "solution" to this mystery...

[55] *The Philadelphia Inquirer* (Philadelphia, PA), December 3, 1906.

So, was it a crazed man or a dog? Let's get our stories straight, officers! A man, wrapped in bearskin, is agile enough to perform all of the feats attributed to this creature? A man is able to run, fast as a racehorse, on all fours? The detail of the phosphorous in his hair is a nice addition - unfortunately, none of the other reports mention glowing hair. Where is the proof of these allegations that this "crazy" man did all of the things the detective is claiming in this article? How does the detective know he did all of these things? This too seems like an attempt to either calm the community or for Detective Wagner to live up to his job title by "solving" the mystery.

[56] *Reporter* (Eureka, UT), December 7, 1906.

[57] Illustration from the article below, "Strange Monster Scares Citizens" *The Spanish Fork Press* (Spanish Fork, UT) December 27, 1906.

[58] *The Spanish Fork Press* (Spanish Fork, UT) December 27, 1906.

[59] *The Fulton County News* (McConnellsburg, PA) August 1, 1907.

[60] *Reading Times* (Reading, PA) August 27, 1907.

[61] *Daily News Standard* (Uniontown, PA) August 27, 1907.

[62] *Pittsburgh Post-Gazette* (Pittsburgh, PA) October 27, 1907.

There have been a few modern sightings of white-haired bigfoot creatures in Pennsylvania - this apparition seems to indicate white-haired creatures have been seen in Pennsylvania for many years.

[63] *Reading Times* (Reading, PA) March 19, 1908.

[64] *Pittsburgh Daily Post* (Pittsburgh, PA) May 17, 1908.

[65] *Pittsburgh Daily Post* (Pittsburgh, PA) August 16, 1908.

[66] *The York Daily* (York, PA) January 30, 1909.

[67] *The Danville Morning News* (Danville, PA) April 13, 1909.

[68] *Wilkes-Barre Times Leader, The Evening News* (Wilkes-Barre, PA) June 14, 1909.

An unsolved murder, bare footprints in deep snow, a wild-man, mysterious screams, strange lights, and a haunting: Again we see the motif of multiple strange phenomena happening in the same time and place.

[69] *Wilkes-Barre Times Leader, The Evening News* (Wilkes-Barre, PA) June 14, 1909.

"Peeper" stories are not usually among my searches when looking for possible historic bigfoot reports. Bigfoot are known for peering in windows, but the search results tend to be flooded with common peeping toms. That said, this story appears directly below the above "wild man" story in the newspaper and it caught my eye. A woman, dressed in black, peeping through windows, and somehow able to evade capture by an entire police force aided by 100 citizens! A woman who easily "shakes off" several men and vaults high fences! Perhaps there is something more to this woman in black. I find it doubly interesting that it should be printed alongside a wild man story.

[70] *The Wellsboro Gazette* (Wellsboro, PA) June 23, 1909.

[71] *The Wilkes-Barre News* (Wilkes-Barre, PA) July 19, 1909.

[72] *The Gettysburg Times* (Gettysburg, PA) October 4, 1909.

[73] *Harrisburg Telegraph* (Harrisburg, PA) October 9, 1909.

[74] *Harrisburg Telegraph* (Harrisburg, PA) October 14, 1909.

VII. AN UNKNOWN MONSTER

1910 - 1919

ARRESTED AS WILD MAN; DENIES CHARGE

ROCHESTER, Pa., June 4. — East Rochester borough is having a wild man scare. A real wild man with hair almost knee length, long scrawly claws that answered for fingers, is said to have been prowling around through thickets, occasionally coming out into the open and frightening women and children, as well as brave men, nearly out of their wits. The reign of terror has been in session for the past few days. Yesterday, a man who gave his name as Crawford Emerick, no occupation, was arrested by Constable Allkine, on charge of being the wild man. Although he answered fairly well to the description, Justice Simpson of East Rochester, who saw the alleged wild man, said he wasn't it. Emerick is being held in jail as being a suspicious character.[1]

———◆———

According to the Williamsport News a wild man was seen along Coudersport pike. *The Pottsville Journal* miscreant has been off the job for some time. That's probably the answer.[2]

———◆———

STRANGE MONSTER DODGES BULLETS

BINDNAGLE'S CHURCH MYSTERY BAFFLES A PARTY OF HUNTERS.

SCOFFERS WON'T BELIEVE.

Say the Only Wild Animal There is The Chipmunk. — Searching Party Sees the Animal Terror in The Swatara.

A party composed of fifteen men and boys, all of them armed, set out in quest of the strange animal that is alleged to have its lair in a cavern along the Swatara creek near Bindnagle's Church, the other night. The net result of the expedition is that one member of the party claims that he got a glimpse of the mysterious monster and fired a shot at it and missed.

That is, he presumes that he failed to hit the beast as he claims that it shook its head savagely and ran away. Another member of the party verifies this story and says the animal disappeared in Adam Boltz's meadow.

This morning another party, comprising twenty men, visited the vicinity of the cave. While several were watching the place, a cry was heard, and the watchers turned and saw the creature bathing in the Swatara, a short distance south of where they were standing.

Several shots were fired, but all were without effect. Members of this party describe the creature as an animal weighing between 200 and 300 pounds, light in color, and having a sandy head.

Mr. Maulfair, a reputable citizen, asserts that he has seen the mysterious visitor running about in Mr. Rasp's meadow, between the Swatara and the Quittapahilla.

At one farm in the vicinity the heads of twenty-three chickens were found. Some lay the slaughter to the beast, and others say that it would not take the bodies and leave the heads. Others claim that they have watched the cave on the Swatara and have seen nothing in the shape of an animal in that vicinity except chipmunks.[3]

An Unknown Monster

The report is current in Russell that a large animal of an unknown species has taken up its abode in the woods between Porter's Point and Putnamville. Several persons claim to have seen it on different occasions. It is described as being tall, somewhat like a man with large fiery eyes and gives vent to blood curdling shrieks when approached. The appearance of the monster in that quiet neighborhood is causing a great deal of comment and speculation.[4]

───────◆───────

YOUTHS CHASED BY A WILD MAN

Perry Countians Stirred Up By Mountain Maniac

CHESTNUT HUNTERS SCARED

Residents Along Mountain From Marysville to Duncannon Tell of Seeing Hairy Human Being Whose Words Are Unintelligible.

Cove, Pa., Oct. 3 — All the residents along the mountain from Marysville to Duncannon, are stirred up over the sudden appearance of a wild man. He was first seen Sunday and since then he has appeared before several travelers over the Cove mountains. One and all describe the wild man as being a repulsive, dirty, ragged, and uncouth person, attired in tatters and apparently dulled to all human sensibilities.

While hunting chestnuts in the Cove mountains Sunday, George and Charles Barnett and Harry Shaver climbed to the topmost point of this place. They were busy swinging their clubs, trying to get a few chestnuts, though the nuts were not ripe. They were startled by a sudden apparition.

A big man bounded into their midst and began snatching at the few nuts lying scattered about. The young men looked at him in amazement. He had long black hair, falling over his shoulders; his hairy chest denoted great strength. One thing very peculiar, the nut hunters noticed, was that his eyes were blue, the cerulean hue of the skies.

They didn't wait to inspect this queer personage very long; the description they gave is a composite one, pieced together when they arrived safe at home an hour later. After snatching a few nuts, the wild man gave a preliminary wave of his hands, jumped into the air and cracked his bare heels together and then yelled. The Barnett brothers and Shaver ran.

Over log, through underbrush, leaping small streams, the boys fled on. Wings were lent to their feet by fear as behind them they heard the mutterings and dog-like growlings of their pursuer. Not one intelligible word did the wild man give utterance. Finally, on reaching the road, the youths got their second wind and though they did not stop to look around, they knew they were out-distancing the wild man.

Shaver had a narrow escape, as he tripped once on the flight down the mountainside. With several rolls — he never stopped long enough to arise naturally — he got to his feet and soon caught up with the flying Barnetts.

Two Marysville men saw the wild man yesterday upon the highest point of the Cove mountains. It is thought that he has his nest up there somewhere. Where he came from and who he is is a mystery to everybody along the mountainside. A searching party now will be made up to capture the man, as some of the farmers fear for their women folk should they be away from the house after dark.[5]

———◆———

A WILD MAN

A half nude man, probably an escaped lunatic, has been seen in the vicinity of Hazleton and scared many ladies. The authorities are searching for him.[6]

———◆———

VALUABLE DOGS STRANGELY LOST

Residents Fear Wild Man Is Prowling About Country

Marietta, Nov. 2. — This community yesterday was thrown into some excitement when a report was circulated that a wild man or beast was in the vicinity. A. R. McKein, who resides at the extreme end of the borough, lost two very valuable dogs and the mystery of their disappearance is puzzling.

Mr. McKein had been up until 1 o'clock yesterday morning filling shells for the purpose of going gunning, and at the time the dogs were in their kennels and chained. About 4 o'clock Mr. McKein in company with his three brothers, Samuel McKein, George McKein, of this place, and Armor McKein, of Lancaster, started out for rabbits, but did not take the dogs along.

When the quartet returned yesterday before noon Mr. McKein noted his loss. Searching for some time in the neighborhood they returned to the house and ransacked the bedding of the dogs and found their collars and the jawbones of both dogs and part of a skull. There are marks on the skull which show that some animal had been biting at it. No one heard any noise. The supposition and from all appearances there is a wild beast in the neighborhood. There are no tracks of any animal, no blood which would show a fight, and not the least identification. The dogs were beagle hounds and were of fine stock.

Some time ago a wild man was seen in the vicinity of Kinderhook, several miles east, and this has so stirred the community that men were walking with clubs and well armed last evening. The quartet scored thirteen rabbits during the day, and all large ones.[7]

---◆---

WILD MAN AT ACCOMAC

Human Being, Entirely Nude, Inhabits River Hills — Chased Girl.

Accomac, June 16. — A supposed wild man was seen in the hills near here, on Friday, by a daughter of Leonard Waller, proprietor of the summer resort, at this place. She was badly frightened by his appearance.

While walking near the water's edge she observed the bare foot of a human being, and upon approaching it, a man, entirely nude, arose and chased her into her home. A search was made immediately, but no one could be found until several hours later, when a man was seen walking down the path and was ordered to leave by Mr. Waller.

Yesterday he was seen in the hills by several visitors from the lower end of the county, who spent the day there.[8]

"Wild" Man Reported

A "wild" man is reported in the Hills near Accomac, across the Susquehanna from Marietta. He is said to be nude and to have long beard and hair. It is believed he is an escaped lunatic.[9]

Hunting For Wild Man

Farmers in the vicinity of Danville for the past week have been badly frightened by a report circulating through the county of the appearance of a strange man who is unkempt and barks like a dog. Women on the farms north of Danville refuse to stay in their homes when the men leave for work in the fields and accompany them. A special policeman has been ordered to search the woods for the wild man by the chief of police of Danville.[10]

A wild man who it is believed is demented, is hiding in the Moosic mountains.[11]

Stroudsburg — Farmers of the countryside are searching the woods for a "wild man." The women and children are terror stricken and refuse to leave their homes after dark.[12]

Finding of Skeleton Brings Up Stories of "Wild Man"

Lewistown, Pa., Nov. 3 — Discovery of a human skeleton in the woods a few miles west of McVeytown on Monday evening by a hunter is thought to solve the mystery of a "wild man" who roamed the mountains in this section about ten or twelve years ago. The find was made by John Youtzy, of near this place.

The skeleton was found among some bushes and near by were found faded shreds of clothing hanging to undergrowth. The bones of the skeleton were bleached, but were all there, and were those of a good-sized man.

David Miller, a resident of Oliver township, living near where the find was made, says that the bones are likely those of a man who made his appearance in the neighborhood about a decade ago. He was called a "wild man."[13]

◆

Town Hunts for Wild Man

Danville, Pa., Nov. 16. — Danville people are sleeping with one eye open these nights while the police are hunting for an alleged wild man who is said to be frequenting Mausdale and adjacent territory. According to the stories of young men and women a mysterious person, unclothed, has been making sudden appearance along country roads.[14]

◆

EXCITEMENT CAUSED BY WILD MAN

Danville and territory adjacent thereto seems to be the habitat of uncanny and mysterious personages, who in addition to a sagacity that enables them to elude pursuit, possess an aversion to conventional attire, even if on occasion they do not discard all clothing and appear as Adam before the fall. It was only a trifle over a year ago, when the residents of South Danville were terrorized by a "wild man" who periodically sallied forth and each time mysteriously disappeared at the moment pursuit was organized. More recently an apparition, guiltless of clothing in any form, according to report, haunted the bushes in the vicinity of the idle steel plant at the eastern end of the borough. The sensation caused by the reports of the periodical appearance will easily be recalled. Now unless the evidence of reputable witnesses is not to be regarded, the "wild man" has made his appearance in the vicinity of Mausdale, his make up — or utter lack of it — being such as to inspire quite as much fear and aversion as on any of his previous visits.

The strange animal is at present terrorizing Mausdale, and may or may not be the one who haunted the bushes at the steel plant last summer and at an earlier date appeared in South Danville. He appears to have been in hiding on the slope of the ridges just west of Hunter's Creek, where there is a dense growth of evergreens. For a full week he has periodically appeared at the forks of the road just below and his appearance is described as simply picturesque and scandalous in the extreme.[15]

---◆---

EAST END WILD MAN ON THE JOB AGAIN

Depraved Specimen of Humanity Who Created Consternation Last Year.

The "wild man" who affects a style of dress resembling "Adam before the fall," has made his periodical appearance in the bushes in the vicinity of the old steel plant. Last year about this time a similar apparition created consternation at the same spot, appearing on several different occasions. He managed to elude the police as well as several citizens living near, who aided in an attempt to run the fellow down.

On Thursday, the man, nude, was seen on practically the same spot where he was wont to disport himself last summer by a woman living in Gulick's Addition. Learning of the affair Emil J. LeDue and one or more of his employees dropped their work at the greenhouse and went over to the bushes to look for the man, who as on previous occasions was smart enough to effect a get-away.

Yesterday morning the matter was reported to Officer Voris, whose beat lies in that part of town. From now on the fellow will have to be pretty vigilant, if he succeeds in escaping capture.[16]

---◆---

TROOPERS SEEK WILD MAN SEEN NEAR HARVEYS LAKE

WILKES-BARRE, Feb. 28. — The mysterious wild man; who has terrorized girls in the Harveys Lake section, is still at large. State Trooper Gallagher is in charge of a squad of men that is trying to run him down.

The mysterious man was seen late Monday night and gave chase to a young woman and her escort. All the young men of Harveys Lake, who have courage enough to go out at night, are armed.[17]

---◆---

SOUTH SIDE HAS WILD MAN SCARE

Evidently a Depraved Specimen Who Delights in Keeping the Community Stirred Up.

TERRORIZES YOUNG WOMEN

South Siders Owe it to Their Wives and Daughters to Get Rid of This Brute.

There are few communities that are not afflicted with the traditional "Wild Man." About this time of year annually or there about one makes his appearance at Danville, much to the consternation of the women and children. A few years ago the South Siders were terrorized. Later an apparition appeared in the bushes near the abandoned Steel plant at the East End. Now again it is the South Side that is terrorized. In all instances the wild man seems to manifest a repugnance to raiment and appears as nearly as possible like "Adam before the Fall."

So far as the reappearance of the monster on the South Side at this time is concerned the story is well authenticated. A reputable young woman had an experience with the brute as late as Sunday night. She was very badly frightened but managed to escape. A few days before another young woman, of unquestioned veracity, was very badly frightened by the fellow. If any of the South Siders have been disposed to regard these stories as fairy tells they had better disabuse their minds and get their guns.

Of course, no person with any sense would take any stock in the "Wild Man" theory. What they have at large on the South Side is some ordinary low-down specimen, who delights in keeping the community stirred up and in gratifying his own depraved instincts.

The people of the south side owe it to their wives and daughters to get rid of this human brute and they should lose no time about it. It is preposterous to assume that he can not be captured, if the right methods are employed. Let the whole community get after him. No clemency should be shown the fellow: let him take whatever punishment falls to his lot.[18]

———◆———

A wild man has been roaming over Twolick hills for a couple weeks.[19]

―――――◆―――――

HAIRY WILD MAN LOOSE IN LEIPERVILLE SECTION, CRIES OO-OO AND MAG MAG!

Fisherman Along Ridley Creek See Strange Creature Whose Savage Appearance and Weird Calls Are as Blood Curdling as Pitiful, So They Tell Startled Village on Return From Notable Adventure

CHESTER, Pa., Sept 3. — A wild man is roaming around in the section of Delaware county adjacent to Leiperville and through Ridley township, according to the story brought into the village this morning by Hugh Duffy, John Wiley, Mike Dillon and Lawrence Scott, a quartette of fishermen who took a day off to angle for carp in Ridley Creek, near Avondale.

The four men tell the same story in the same way about the strange creature they saw hopping around on all-fours, pawing the earth and going through pantomimic antics. He gives vent to piteous "oo-oo" and cries out in a guttural, but loud and distinct voice. "Mag-Mag-Mag." These are the only two sounds he makes.

Duffey, Wiley, Dillon, and Scott are employed at the Eddystone plant of the Baldwin Locomotive Works, and have lived in Leiperville for a number of years. All are known to be truthful, sober men. One by one the perturbed anglers gave an account of their experience, and so great was the thrill and sensation thrown into the villagers that many of them declared they would put double locks and strong bars upon their doors and windows before going to bed tonight.

The women folks are especially worked up over the stories of the returning fishermen, and are more susceptible to the hair-bristling accounts of the wild man than are the men, who organized hunting party this afternoon and went to look for the strange creature. At nightfall they had not found him.

Anyone having felt the blood-curdling effect of the awful "oo-oo" will never want to hear it again, aver both Wiley and Duffy, but the pronunciation of his second call, that of "Mag-Mag," is still more ghostly and ominous as the strange being keeps hopping about the bushes and tall grasses. The name "Mag" is believed to be that of a woman for whom either in fact or in fancy the wild man is looking.

Lawrence Scott says he was so badly rattled that he was speechless.

"Of all the hideous animals, it was that wild man," declared Wiley. "He had hair all over his face and it hung a foot from his chin, and he went jumping among the rocks just like a bear, and every minute he would poke his devilish head above the bushes and yell "oo-oo." Then we would lose sight of the old fellow, when he would suddenly pop up his head and yell, "Mag-Mag." Why, the cries were so pitiful they went clean through me."

Some believe the strange creature is a man who escaped from some institution. As for the four men who claim they saw the "Wild Man," they cannot be shaken in their story and are firm in their belief that the frightful being is wandering through the country in search of an old sweetheart, maybe, who probably spurned his love and drove him crazy.[20]

◆

Some kind of wild man has been making his home in local cornfields in day time and sleeping in stables at night. He acts like a person who is mentally unbalanced, but there are also those who think that he may be a thieves spy.[21]

◆

According to the *Carnegie Signal-Item* there were two bears in Carnegie the other day while at nights a gorilla is prowling around the suburbs seeking whom it may catch and devour. Why shouldn't Brother Bnepper of the S.-I. organize a menagerie and tour the South during the winter?[22]

◆

"Wild Man," Strikes Terror Into Greene County Folk

WAYNESBURG, PA., Dec. 20 — A "wild man" at large in the vicinity of Ryerson station, Richill township, is terrorizing the section, according to reports to county authorities. The man was seen yesterday by Homer Campbell, who resides near the Guthrie school. He was hiding in a clump of briars.

Campbell went to summon

help but the man had gone when he returned. Later he was seen near the residence of J. M. Lazear but escaped into a dense wood.[23]

———◆———

[1] *New Castle News* (New Castle, PA) June 4, 1910.

[2] *The Allentown Democrat* (Allentown, PA) October 4, 1910.

[3] *Lebanon Courier and Semi-Weekly Report* (Lebanon, PA) October 21, 1910.

[4] *Evening Mirror* (Lebanon, PA) July 13, 1911.

[5] *Harrisburg Daily Independent* (Harrisburg, PA) October 3, 1911.

[6] *Mount Carmel Item* (Mount Carmel, PA) September 9, 1912.

[7] *Harrisburg Daily Independent* (Harrisburg, PA) November 2, 1912.

[8] *The York Daily* (York, PA) June 17, 1913.
    The Accomac Inn is said to be haunted. It also sits in the Hellam Hills a very short distance from Toad Road, a major subject of my first book *Beyond the Seventh Gate*, where I have collected several encounters with bigfoot creatures - and things exhibiting known bigfoot behavior.

[9] *The Courier* (Harrisburg, PA) June 22, 1913.

[10] *Wilkes-Barre Semi-Weekly Record* (Wilkes-Barre, PA) September 30, 1913.

[11] *Wilkes-Barre Times Leader, The Evening News* (Wilkes-Barre, PA) September 8, 1914.

[12] *The Evening News* (Wilkes-Barre, PA) May 20, 1915.

[13] *Harrisburg Telegraph* (Harrisburg, PA) November 3, 1915.

[14] *Harrisburg Daily Independent* (Harrisburg, PA) November 16, 1915.

[15] *Mount Carmel Item* (Mount Carmel, PA) November 16, 1915.

[16] *The Danville Morning News* (Danville, PA) August 19, 1916.

[17] *The Evening News* (Harrisburg, PA) February 28, 1917.

[18] *The Danville Morning News* (Danville, PA) June 21, 1918.

[19] *The Indiana Weekly Messenger* (Indiana, PA) August 7, 1919.

[20] *The Philadelphia Inquirer* (Philadelphia, PA) September 4, 1919.
   It is doubtful that a single human, however unusual, could inspire the kind of fear reported by the anglers in this article. Many modern bigfoot witnesses, upon hearing the cries of the creature, state that they never want to hear them again.

[21] *Lebanon Daily News* (Lebanon, PA) September 29, 1919.

[22] *The Daily Notes* (Canonsburg, PA) October 11, 1919.

[23] *Pittsburgh Post Gazette* (Pittsburgh, PA) December 21, 1919.

VIII. GORILLA ATTACKS

THE 1920'S

REPORT "WILD MAN" AT LARGE.

Waynesburg, Pa., Jan. 2 — A "wild man" is reported at large in the rough country near here. He has been seen a number of times, but all efforts to capture him have failed. People living near the scene are excited over the appearance of the stranger and keep close to their houses.[1]

◆

GORILLA CAUSES TERROR IN TOWNS

Takes Up Residence in Mine at Doerr Terrace.

New Homestead and Doerr Terrace in Mifflin township were the scenes of much excitement yesterday over the rumor that a gorilla or large ape had taken up its abode in an abandoned coal mine on the hillside in Doerr Terrace. The animal was first reported to have been seen Tuesday evening by Mrs. William Jenkins and Walter West of Doerr Terrace.

It has caused a number of scares to persons in the district, at night, at which time, it is said, it leaves the abandoned mine and saunters about in search of food. Homer Wozley, of Mifflin township, reported that the animal followed him Thursday night almost to the doorstep of his home.

Last evening a party of searchers, armed with weapons, attempted to rout the animal from the mine, but owing to the entrance being swampy it was decided to wait outside at the mouth of the mine until the animal decided to take its usual stroll.[2]

◆

GORILLA HUNT BEING WAGED IN MIFFLIN TWP.

Electric searchlights will be used by residents of Mifflin township today to explore the abandoned mine near New Homestead in which it is reported a gorilla or ape has taken up his abode, sallying forth from time to time for food.

Boys and men armed with rifles and shotguns have been watching the mine entrance since yesterday to trap the animal.

Nick Broeski entered the mine late last night in a search for the gorilla. He could not find it but brought out the torn body of an animal thought to be a sheep.

Women and children in the neighborhood are terrorized and to definitely determine whether there is a gorilla in the mine a posse will enter the workings this evening with searchlights and rifles.[3]

◆

MYSTERIOUS GORILLA IN MIFFLIN TOWNSHIP MILKS EIGHT COWS!

Not content with a diet of fruit and vegetables stolen from gardens in the West Homestead and Mifflin township district, the big gorilla which has been terrorizing Negroes in that district is thought to have sallied forth from his supposed hiding place in an abandoned mine yesterday afternoon, and milked eight cows pasturing in the vicinity. No one actually saw the animal in the act, as far as is known, but the farmers to whom the cows belong are reported to place the blame for the theft of the milk on the simian marauder and have joined the gorilla hunt.

How the animal escaped from the mine yesterday except by some side entry, it is believed by Nick Proto and Peter Delanto, members of the posse who kept an all-day vigil with loaded rifles at the mouth of the mine yesterday while others explored the accessible parts with electric searchlights. It is believed the activities of the searching party around the mouth of the mine and the shooting by several foreigners Friday night when they imagined they saw the gorilla caused it to slink back into some remote part of the mine and find another way to escape.

Several of the farmers whose cows came home milkless and who were forced to drink their coffee black last night expressed their intention of keeping their cows under observation today for the purpose of determining just how a gorilla goes about the operation of milking a cow.[4]

The Man Ape Who Had Terrorized the Whole City.

5

ARMED POSSE OF 100 HUNTS FOR HUGE APE IN ABANDONED MINE

Mifflin Township and New Homestead Residents Join in search for Animal — Bullets Menace Hunters in Sark Shaft — Many persons See Gorilla.

Mifflin township and New Homestead, declaring an open season on the bipeds which Darwin made famous, went ape-hunting last night. No fewer than 100 men and boys, each equipped with a revolver or shotgun, invaded an abandoned coal mine between Hays borough and Homestead., firing frequent volleys into the impenetrable darkness in efforts to bag the big ape or gorilla which is said to have made the district his (or her) habitat for several days.

However, the much-sought animal evaded capture. Perhaps he lay in some sequestered nook in the murky workings of the old mine, or perhaps he was frisking through the dense brush on mountain-like Doerr's Terrace. At all events, he was not at home to the energetic "posse."

The lives of the relentless hunters, as they searched the interior of the old mine, were in more or less danger as the flying bullets frequently dislodged slate, which fell in showers in the passages. Rays from electric searchlights glinted and flickered through the gloomy lanes.

There are many who claim to have seen the ape in the district. Two Negro boys told an earnest tale of having glimpsed the animal in a tree on the terrace. Others reported having seen him flee in terror as workmen approached him in a New Homestead street. Nick Broeski, a farmer, explored the old mine early yesterday and came forth with the torn body of a sheep. This was accepted as exhibit A in the case against the ape.

The fruitless search will be continued, the hunters say.[6]

◆

No Gorilla — But!

It Was a Bad Day for Household Pets.

A shetland pony belonging to a resident of West Homestead had several narrow escapes from death yesterday at the hands of the gorilla hunters who scoured the underbrush in the vicinity of Homestead Park in search for the gorilla that is believed to be living in the neighborhood. Dogs, rabbits, cats and other animals moving in the weeds and underbrush also furnished short-lived thrills for the hunters.

That people living within a radius of several miles of the reported haunts of the gorilla are taking the stories seriously was evidenced yesterday by the absence of small children alone in the fields, as well as the scarcity of berry pickers in the blackberry thickets. Farmers whose cows came home milkless Sunday guarded their pastures yesterday with shotguns.[7]

◆

SHOOTING ON "SUSPICION."

Gorilla Not Exactly Seen, But Shots Are Fired.

Shots were fired again last night in Mifflin township's "gorilla chase." Excited guards watching cattle and sheep are said to have fired the shots on "suspicion."

Many persons were out until late last night in hopes of glimpsing the gorilla which is reported to have been prowling about for several days, but none reported having seen it. Excitement over the affair is gradually dying out and today residents of the district are beginning to look upon the matter as a hoax.⁸

It is reported that a large gorilla running at large near Pittsburgh milked eight cows a few nights ago. Those chaps who have stills are greatly alarmed as a gorilla with an appetite like that could lick up the contents of many stills every night.⁹

Why go to Africa when you can hunt a gorilla near New Homestead?¹⁰

TONY NOT GORILLA MAN, GIRLS ATTACKED SAY.

Tony Ruzicka, aged 35, thought by some to have been the "gorilla" which has caused apprehension in Mifflin and Baldwin townships, last night was acquitted of a charge of vagrancy, at a hearing before Justice of the Peace Walter Terrill of Hays. Ruzicka agreed to leave the district.

An attempt was made to connect the man with an attack on Monday on Miss Anna Shaffer, aged 21, of Baldwin township. Miss Shaffer and her younger sister, confronting Ruzicka, said he was not the man who accosted them.

Ruzicka told authorities he had walked most of the way from New York, arriving in Baldwin township yesterday. He was arrested in a wood near Glass Run rd.¹¹

Dr. J. A. Williams, W. G. Wittmer, A. Dundy and Ed Grumenacker of Pittsburgh were coon hunting last evening in the Ginger Hill vicinity. They rounded up 5 coons and would possibly have secured more had they not been frightened by the would be gorilla that is reported loitering around Dry Run. They took shelter at the Nixon home and it is stated "there never were four worse scared men."¹²

Boys After the Gorilla

The boys at McKean's school think they have found the gorilla in an opening of the old Grant mine near the school. The boys are out after it every night. *The Signal-Item* will pay a liberal reward for its capture, dead or alive.[13]

———◆———

Wild Animal Mauls Snyder County Boy

MIDDLEBURG, Dec. 11 — Residents of this part of Snyder County are sleeping with one eye open these nights over a well-authenticated report that a gorilla is at large in the neighborhood and posses were out all day today searching for it.

John Boilig, 12 years old, was caught and badly mauled by the animal as he was going toward his father's stables. He is in critical condition. He describes it as being all hairy and big.

Residents scout the idea that it is a gorilla, but believe the boy may have been attacked by a wildcat.[14]

———◆———

Boy Says He Was Attacked by Wild Mountain Beast

Lewistown, Dec. 14 — Declaring that he was attacked by a gorilla last night while cutting wood, the 15-year-old son of Charles Bolig, a farmer living near Meiser, in Snyder county, today is seriously hurt. The boy evidently was attacked by some mountain animal and avers that it looked like a gorilla.

Since the attack became known stories are in circulation here concerning the escape last summer near Williamsport of several circus animals. Motorists declare that they saw such an animal last night near the Lewistown Narrows.[15]

———◆———

LEWISTOWN YOUTH HAS THRILLING EXPERIENCE.

Lewistown, Dec. 14 — Knocked down and badly beaten by a huge animal believed to have been a circus gorilla, Samuel Boling, 15 year old son of Mr. and Mrs. Robert Boling, near here, is still unconscious today. The boy about two weeks ago wounded the animal, and it is believed it followed him to his home and with almost human intelligence, awaited an opportunity to attack him.[16]

---◆---

GORILLA BADLY INJURES BOY AT LEWISTOWN

Lewistown, Pa., Dec. 14 — Knocked down and badly beaten by a huge animal believed to have been an escaped circus gorilla, Samuel Bolling, the 15 year old son of Mr. and Mrs. Robert Bolling, near here is still unconscious today. The boy wounded the animal about two weeks ago and it is believed it followed him to his home and with almost human intelligence awaited its first opportunity to attack him.

Late last night the boy stepped outside the kitchen door. A few minutes later members of the family were aroused by his screams. The father, armed with an axe, ran to ascertain the trouble. As he approached the boy, writhing in pain on the ground, he saw a huge animal, traveling first on two feet and then on four, make its escape in the darkness.

The boy murmured something about "the big animal more than feet high" and then became unconscious. He is so badly beaten and mutilated that it is feared he will not regain consciousness.

Members of the family and nearby residents have seen the huge animal on several occasions. Young Bolling, accompanied by his twin sister, Margaret, saw the animal two months ago and told members of the family about it. Two weeks ago, while hunting and armed with a 22 calibre rifle the boy saw the animal in a corn field and fired at it. With companions he traced it through the woods for several hundred yards by a trail of blood left behind.

It has not been seen since from that time until last night when it attacked young Bolling. Members of the family believed it followed his trail to his home awaiting its first chance at vengeance for the wound it suffered. An animal believed to have been a gorilla was reported to have escaped from a carnival at Williamsport last summer and was later seen near here.[17]

---◆---

ESCAPED GORILLA ATTACKS AND MAIMS BOY

LEWISTOWN, Dec. 14 — Terribly maimed by a wild animal, supposed to have been an escaped circus gorilla, the 15-year-old son of Mr. and Mrs. Charles Boling, of Meiser, Snyder County, is unconscious at the home of his parents.

The boy, with his father, early this morning, was in the woods chopping wood, the boy some little distance away from his father, when the father heard a terrible scream.

Rushing to the boy the father found him covered with blood and lying on the ground. The boy murmured something about a big animal, more than seven feet high, and then sank into an unconscious state from which he has not yet been revived.

It is thought that the beast may have escaped from a circus at Williamsport last Summer, and which is supposed to be roaming through the woods in this section.

Another theory is that the animal was a bear. Physicians say the boy has a chance to recover.[18]

―――――◆―――――

GIANT GORILLA CREATES FEAR IN SNYDER COUNTY

Animal Believed To Have Escaped From Carnival Breaks Boy's Arm During Attack — Had Previously Been Wounded

VISITS BOLIG FARM QUITE OFTEN

The appearance of a man ape or gorilla in the mountains of Snyder county has caused great excitement among the residents of the section where the animal was seen. The big ape was first seen three weeks ago by Samuel Bolig, of Meiser, a small town in Snyder county. The animal is supposed to be one that escaped some time ago from a carnival and which has since been living in the mountains of that section of the state.

Samuel and Margaret Bolig, the children of Charles Bolig, were gathering kindling wood one night in November, with the light of a search lamp, when a huge animal about seven feet tall and that stood up like a man, was discovered by the children within the circle of light. It looked to them like a huge monkey and when discovered dropped on all fours and ambled away, soon disappearing in the darkness.

A week later the same animal was discovered in a corn field on the Bolig farm, which is at the foot of the mountain. Samuel procured a 32-calibre rifle and took a shot at the huge man creature, evidently wounding it, as it fell at the shot, rolling over several times on the ground. The boy and his father trailed the wounded ape some distance by the blood but were unable to overtake it, and at length gave up the pursuit.

On Monday night of the present week the strange creature made its third appearance at the Bolig farm. Charles Bolig was engaged in chopping wood by the light of a lantern when the ape approached near enough to be seen. The son ran to the house and procured the rifle but before he could shoot the gorilla viciously attacked him, knocking him down and breaking his arm, and was finally driven away by the father. The lad lay on the ground in an unconscious condition. He was taken to the house and soon after recovered his senses and it was found that he was not seriously injured. He suffered much from shock but is expected to be fully recovered in a short time.

A large number of men armed with rifles started out to hunt the animal; about one hundred Lewistown hunters are scouring the Narrows and surrounding country, toward the Snyder county line, in the hope of getting a shot at the huge creature and killing it, as its presence has caused the greatest consternation in that section, the gorilla being a very dangerous animal on account of its great size, strength and savage nature.[19]

———◆———

ON HUNT FOR MYSTERY ANIMAL

The appearance of a strange animal in the vicinity of Lewistown, Mifflin County, which is said closely to resemble an ape, and which has attacked and injured one boy, has aroused the entire community.

The animal has been seen on several occasions, but usually at night and not distinctly enough for anyone to give a complete description.

Yesterday at least a hundred men, heavily armed, were scouring the countryside in search of the beast.

The supposed ape was seen for the first time about three weeks ago by Samuel Bolig, 15-year-old son of Charles Bolig, at his home in Meiserville, just over the Snyder County line.

On this occasion the boy had gone to the woodpile close to his home at night and with the aid of a pocket searchlight was gathering up kindling wood.

Boy Shoots At It

The beast appeared then in the rays of the light. The boy, frightened, grabbed up his little sister who had accompanied him and fled into his home. A further search by members of the family revealed nothing, and little credence was given the story that he told.

A few days afterward the boy came upon the animal again in the day time. This time, the story goes he was armed with a 32-calibre rifle. He shot at it as it was running through a cornfield. The shots took effect and he was able to track the beast for some distance by the trail of blood until it reached a wooded district where the trail was lost.

Nothing further was seen of the animal until last Sunday night when it appeared again at the Bolig home. The Bolig boy and his father were gathering kindling on the same woodpile when the beast came into the rays of the searchlight.

Father Also Sees It

As the father held the animal at bay the boy ran to his home and secured a revolver. He returned and walked up to the beast to get a good shot when it leaped upon him. The gun was knocked from his hand and he was thrown to the ground, breaking his arm. The father of the boy swung at the animal with an axe but missed it. It then disappeared.

This story was verified yesterday in Lewistown by the father of the boy, Charles Bolig.

When these reports were confirmed yesterday afternoon by Bolig, excitement gripped the whole community. Outside of the town parents refused to allow their children to go far from their homes. Gunning parties have been sent out to kill the beast.

It was reported yesterday that it was seen in the mountains of the Lewistown narrows.

Various stories are in circulation as to just what kind of animal has been creating the disturbance. The boy declares that it resembles a giant monkey.

Others think that it is a gorilla, one that is said to have escaped from a circus that was showing at Williamsport last Summer. Some think that it is a bear.[20]

———◆———

GORILLA ATTACKS AUTOIST LATEST STORY

New stories concerning the mysterious animal that looks like a gorilla and makes a noise like a horse, which has been seen in the lower end of Snyder County during the past month, are in circulation every hour of the day there and the tale of an alleged attack upon an autoist South of Selinsgrove is today's best tale.

The gorilla, or whatever the animal terror may turn out to be leaped upon an autoist traveling toward Selinsgrove. So the story goes, and he would no doubt have been badly done up, but for his resistance with a small penknife, which was the only weapon at hand.

When the fight was at its height, according to the story, another autoist came along and joined in the fray, the two automobile drivers succeeding in beating off the animal's attack.

Exhaustive investigation failed to reveal the names of the autoists or other particulars of the incident.[21]

---◆---

WILD APE ROAMING IN BLAIR COUNTY

Altoona, Pa., Dec. 18 — The wild ape which has been cutting capers in Snyder county is believed to have transferred its scene of operations to Blair county. Samuel Brannen of Canoe Creek, is reported to have seen a strange animal resembling an ape near his home, but it disappeared when he went for his shotgun. It had previously scared his son.

The same night, Mike Sutlige, an Austrian, who lives nearby, met the creature on a road and raced to the home of a neighbor, not even stopping to open the door, but just burst into the house.

Two pieces of meat were taken from the smokehouse on George Mattern's farm in that vicinity. One piece, partially eaten, was found not far away.[22]

---◆---

APE STILL AT LARGE

The ape, gorilla or whatever sort of animal or freak it may be, which was seen at Canoe Creek last week by Chalmer Brannen and Mike Sutlige, is still at large, so far as the public in general knows, for despite the fact that a still hunt has been made throughout the community, not a single trace of it has been found.[23]

BETTER WATCH OUT OR THE APE MAN'LL GET YOU

HOLLIDAYSBURG, Dec. 19. — Great excitement prevails at present in town over the report that the big gorilla, that escaped last summer from a carnival at Williamsport, and recently appeared at a farm in Snyder township, where it broke a boy's arm, and last week was seen at Canoe Creek, in now prowling about Hollidaysburg. Some kind of animal supposed to be the gorilla broke into a smoke house and ate some of the meat on a farm back of Chimney Rocks.

Residents of Loop Station claim to have seen it on Friday night, and a report is current that it was seen at Roselawn, Hollidaysburg, on Saturday night, trying to get into a chicken coop. Better watch out or the ape man will get you. This is especially directed to the small boys who roam about the streets until a late hour, and maybe the presence of the gorilla will have a better effect in this respect than a curfew law.[24]

MORE EVIDENCE SHOWS GIANT SIMIAN STILL ACTIVE IN REGION

Manning Farm Residents Find Imprint on Coop Floor

GOBBLED UP HENS

Strange Footprints Seen Denting Mud at Creek Bank

SWAINS ARMED

Town Lovers of Rural Girls Visit With Qualms

HOLLIDAYSBURG, Dec. 20. — The escaped gorilla that has been prowling about Hollidaysburg and vicinity for the past several days, has a great fondness for chicken, as is evidenced by the fact that it has invaded several coops at night and feasted to its heart's content on the tender juicy meat. The big animal visited the Manning farm at the west end of Chimney Rocks, on Sunday night and broke into the chicken coop, where it enjoyed a royal feast on fifteen fine hens, afterwards taking a siesta on a pile of straw. In the morning when a member of the family visited the coop, the place was found to be littered with feathers and blood, and on the straw was a depression where the ape man had slept.

At Roselawn, the beast's footprints were seen the latter part of last week, in the soft mud near the Brush Run and it was at first supposed to be a bear but was later seen by several persons, who declare it was of the shape of a huge ape. It broke into the chicken coop of George Brenner and Mike Wiseman, and feasted on a number of choice fowls.

The town is all agog over the appearance of the animal, and the boys and girls are keeping close to the house after nightfall. The young men whose girls reside in the rural districts, are making their nightly visits to their sweethearts all cranked up ready to shoot into "high" if the dreaded monster appears in their path. Most of the swains are armed with revolvers, but they might as well shoot at the big creature with a pop gun, unless using a weapon of great power and large calibre, as the gorilla is one of the most powerful of all wild animals. Its muscles are like iron and the bullet from an ordinary revolver would do it little or no harm. The gorilla is so powerful and ferocious that even the lion will retreat before it, and there is no other animal in the African jungle that will face it. This creature has such great strength in its arms, that it can tear a large branch from a tree with the greatest of ease and crush a man like an eggshell. If the unwelcome visitor remains in this section, a concerted movement will be made to hunt it down and kill it, as its presence here is a great menace to the safety of the people.[25]

——————◆——————

ELDORADO YOUNG MEN SEE GORILLA

Pass Great Ape In Road Near Cross Keys

Hearing a slight noise on the road ahead, as though something or someone was coming through the bushes into the road, Lester Bucher and Chester Fink of Eldorado, who were coming down the long hill from Duncansville to Cross Keys at 10 o'clock last night in Fink's automobile, sounded the horn and gazed to the side of the road as they passed the object, only to be horrified as the spotlight crossed the thing to find it a brown colored animal, between six and seven feet tall and standing erect beside the road facing them.

Almost senseless with fear, Fink shoved the gears into high and the car rapidly left the supposed jungle denizen behind. As the automobile got a few feet beyond the thing it emitted a horrid yell, which the young men describe as "loud and coarse." Neither had a gun and for this reason no further attempt at investigation was made. Talking of the incident later, young Bucher said that they both got a good look at the thing as the light played on it and they have no doubt but that it was a gorilla or an animal closely resembling it.[26]

———————◆———————

Narrows Tower Man With Megaphone Gets Answer

RESIDENTS SHIVER

Octogenarian Brands Animal "Satan Unchained"

FEW SAY PANTHER

Christmas Tree Cutting Nil — Ape Fear is Reason

LEWISTOWN, Dec. 20 — Canoe Creek, Blair county, may have imported an alien gorilla or ape-man for its own convenience, but it can't take any of the lustre from Snyder and Mifflin counties which have a prior claim by right of original discovery. All of Saturday night the wild cries of the ape-man that attacked little Sammy Bolig near his home along the mountains near Meiser one week ago and beat him into insensibility echoed from the knob that forms the eastern bank of Macedonia Hollow on the state road side of the Lewistown Narrows. A score or more of railroad men who work in the Denholm yards of the Pennsylvania railroad listened to the cries for hours and vowed that nothing akin to it had ever been heard in the mountains in that section.

They describe the cry as being a cross between that of a child in distress, magnified a thousand fold, and that of Dante's description of the wail of a lost soul. Its volume is something wonderful, the cries being echoed for miles across the mountains.

The cries at first were heart just across the Juniata river from MI signal tower and receded as if the animal was traveling across the knob in the direction of Middleburg. When on the eve of disappearing, M. C. Hack, a sign man, obtained a megaphone and gave the far-famed "call of the woods" as known to the mountain folk in the valley, the animal immediately answered by a shrill scream. Hack continued to call and the animal to answer until it reached a point almost at the foot of the mountain. The passion in the cries made the old-timers, men who have braved the dangers of half a century on the rail, quake in their boots.

The "missing link" hovered about the water's edge for some time, when its cries again showed that it was climbing the knob. The course of the animal could be followed by its wails until they died almost to a whisper in the great distance when one old veteran heaved a sight and remarked, "It's Satan, unchained and abroad. No human animal ever made that noise, leastwise I have never heard it and I have been here nigh onto eighty years."

Some say it's a panther that is sounding the strange cry. One is said to have been sighted near Millerstown a week ago and David Hough, an old mountaineer, residing in Grantville Gap, says a hunter came to his house with a panther cub during the late big game season that was taken back in the Vincent chopping, one of the wildest sections of the Black Log mountain.

Be it the "Missing Link" or only a "What Is It," it has the 'goat' of the mountain folk as well as many others. Its appearance at this time has utterly destroyed the Christmas tree industry in this section, as few have the hardihood to venture into the wilds to cut them with the menace of the gorilla abroad. Science is in favor of the animal instinct leading it south or disposing of it by the pneumonia route in the event of its being a member of the monkey family, while others argue that if it were the escaped member of a circus or carnival it would be accustomed to the human family and would have long since called at lonely habitations along the mountains for food, but these arguments fail utterly to eradicate the fear, either of the natural or supernatural, and even the children are hugging close to the fireside.[27]

GORILLA TERRIFIES MOUNTAIN REGION

Gigantic Ape Attacks People of Hills Near Lewistown.

Philadelphia, Dec. 20 — The reign of terror in the mountain section in the vicinity of Lewistown, Pa., since the advent of a gigantic beast, believed to be an escaped gorilla, has reached such a stage that virtually all activity has been halted.

A week ago the beast attacked a boy named Sammy Bolig. He was beaten insensible by two terrific blows. On Friday a man and his wife returning home in their automobile had a narrow escape when the frightful simian leaped from the brush at the roadside at the auto, They escaped when the man stepped on the accelerator.

Last night, on the state road side of Lewistown Narrows, the animal appeared and set up an unearthly howl. M. C. Hack, a railroad signal man, obtained a megaphone and uttered a long cry through it. Instantly the animal receded into the brush and began screaming and roaring while the railroad workers in the Denham yards listened to the weird duet for hours.[28]

CLAYSBURGERS SEE APE; MIDDLEBURGER TOOK SHOT

CLAYSBURG, Dec. 21 — The escaped carnival ape or some animal of large build was seen in town early this morning not more than a hundred yards from the office of Standard Refractories company. Tracks all around the building show that the animal has feet between ten and twelve inches long and wide in proportion.

At noon today a party of hunters, headed by T. N. Kurtz, president of the refractories company, started out on a hunt for the beast. Thirty men formed the party but this was augmented by almost a hundred others this evening, who, when they were through with their days duties, shouldered high powered rifles and joined in the gorilla hunt.[29]

HOLLIDAYSBURG RESIDENTS BELIEVE GORILLA IS "FROZE UP"

No further news has been received in this section from the gorilla and it is the supposition that big simian perished from the cold on Monday night, being unable to find a place of shelter. On account of being from the tropics, animals of this kind cannot endure very cold weather and the big brute, if it is a gorilla, may have at last succumbed to the icy darts of Jack Frost, which are much more effective than the bullets of mankind.

It would be a great relief to the populace in general to learn that the huge monkey is dead, as its reported presence has taken the whole country by the ears, so that the gorilla is the sole topic of conversation., everyone asking everyone else if they had seen or heard of the terrible creature.

The equanimity of the whole county has been upset, causing many people to stay indoors at night, and preventing visits to and from the rural districts.

A wag says that this must be Tarzan of the apes escaped from the movies, being tired of remaining cooped up in stuffy theatres and wants the freedom of the great outdoors. Be whatever it may, there is surely some strange thing of flesh and blood prowling about.[30]

◆

MIDDLESBURG, Pa., Dec. 21. — While Mr and Mrs. Bruce P. Yeager were driving along a dark road near here Saturday night a huge animal that looked to be seven feet high and to have arms and legs like telegraph poles jumped at their car, missed it and fell sprawling on the road.

Yeager fired two shots at it but the animal made up into the woods and has not been seen since.

Yeager thinks it was the same animal that attacked a boy near Meiser last week, although the spot where it attacked Yeagers is four miles from where the boy lives. It is believed the animal is an ape that escaped from a carnival company at Sunbury last summer.[31]

◆

DRY GAP MAN IS CERTAIN IT'S APE

Claims He Faced Animal at Gaysport Reservoir

"The gorilla is not dead," was the statement of a Dry Gap resident who drove to

Hollidaysburg yesterday for medicine for his sick child — a trip that had been suddenly postponed Christmas night when the same individual started down the lonely mountain road, toward Kladder station, past the Gaysport borough water works.

According to this man, giving his name as Samuel Nedrow, one of his children became ill Saturday afternoon and he decided to come to Kladder, board the 5 o'clock train for Hollidaysburg, get the medicine, and return that far on the outgoing train at 7, walking the distance between his humble mountain home and the station.

He declared that as he neared the Gaysport water works, he heard a barking noise that made his blood run cold. He had never heard anything like it. It was just twilight, and he stopped for an instant to get his bearings. Then again he heard the barking noise. Satisfied the sound was coming from the direction of the reservoir, he started back up the mountain trail.

The racket caused by his running evidently intensified the animal that possessed the barking voice, for he then declared that it turned into a terrific roar. Looking back, Nedrow saw the animal scramble through the bushes, onto the road. He declares he plainly saw a hairy face, practically bare breast, immensely long arms, broad shoulders, but with hind legs very short.

He made no further attempt at investigation. He was unarmed. He had not heard of a gorilla being reported at large, until he came to town and related his experiences, whereupon he declared that he must certainly have seen it. He declares it could not have been a man, and because it stalked on its hind legs, could not have been a bear or any other animal, wild or tame, likely to be found in this climate.

He is of the opinion that it was drinking from the reservoir when it heard him and barked and fumed because disturbed. Nedrow carried a high powered rifle yesterday and if the gorilla should happen to be on his path, he gives assurance he will make this climate hot enough for him, although it is alleged a gorilla could not live in this climate.[32]

———◆———

GORILLA FEAR MAKES HARVEST FOR GARAGE MEN

WILLIAMSBURG, Dec. 27. — The ape scare is proving a veritable windfall for the garage owners of Williamsburg, causing the greenbacks to fairly rain upon them. This is the reason, the foreigners residing in that end of the county, where the men are employed in the various quarries, are deathly afraid of the gorilla, and will not run the risk of getting into the clutches of the terrible beast. So when having occasion to come to Williamsburg, as they often do, they hire automobiles, paying generally five dollars a trip, being afraid to even walk to the nearest railroad station to take the train.

These foreign families keep close to their homes, that are kept closely barred at night by the heavy shutters with which most of the houses are provided. Those shanties that were not equipped with shutters, now have them, as the occupants told their bosses that they would not stay in them unless shutters were provided equipped with strong fasteners.

The men go to their work with fear and trembling, and are greatly relieved when they make the trips safely, expecting at any time to see the hideous monster, which they believe to be lurking in the vicinity. These people would be filled with joy unspeakable if the big ape would be killed, in which event they would have a great jollification, like the jungle men of Africa when a lion or other dangerous beast that has been causing them no end of trouble, has been put to death.[33]

───────◆───────

BETTER THAN CURFEW LAW

The solicitor of one of Blair county's largest boroughs, in discussing the reported appearance of a gorilla in various sections of Blair county, yesterday declared that the reports have had a better effect in keeping youngsters off the streets and highways in the evening than any curfew law that was ever written on the statute books. There has been less complaint about young folks loitering about the streets since these reports have been spread broadcast, he stated, than at any time in years.[34]

───────◆───────

CORRESPONDENT TELLS OF THE "GORILLA SCARE"

Newcomertown, Pa.,
(Middle Spring ave.)
January 12, 1921
Some of the inhabitants of this place and the surrounding territory, especially the timid ones, have been considerably "unnerved" during the past week over the reports that have been current to the effect that a gorilla was "frisking" about in this neck

of the woods."

Rumor after rumor has been noised abroad as to persons seeing the animal resembling a gorilla, but diligent inquiry and investigation by your correspondent has revealed nothing definite and we want to assure the folks in this neighborhood that the stories have absolutely no foundation.

But for the fact that the country is now "bone dry" we would be persuaded that some persons in this section of the country were "seeing things." In the past when "John Barleycorn" held sway it was not uncommon to hear of men seeing snakes and rats, but to the best of our knowledge we never heard of anyone seeing "jungle animals" in this latitude even after imbibing too freely of liquid stronger than the regulation 2 3-4 percent. It may be that our temperance drinks of today — near beer, cider, coca cola, ginger ale, lemon fertilizers, pop, whistle, etc. are responsible for these visions of animals that naturally belong to wild places of darkest Africa.

The first gorilla report came thru the city papers several weeks ago, telling of an encounter a boy in Juniata county had with an animal supposed to have been of that character, which had escaped from a circus and was running at large in the mountains of that region.

Judging from the different places the gorilla has been seen, it would appear that "he" is a very fast walker or is traveling either by auto or aeroplane. Or, it may be that there are a large "flock" of gorillas scampering around the country.

Here are a few of the reports that have been going the rounds the past week, and we want it understood that your correspondent does not vouch for the accuracy of one of them:

The "gorilla" was seen in the mountains near Roxbury and that hunters in that vicinity are organizing to go gunning for it. Now, if this animal is near Roxbury we hope the hunters will succeed in killing or capturing it, but to be on the safe side we would suggest that they first make inquiry of the State Game Warden at Harrisburg as to whether the season for hunting "gorillas" is "In" or "out."

Reports also say that the "gorilla" was seen at Newburg, Middle Spring, Newcomertown, West End, Shippensburg, but what plans have been made for its capture at these points we have been unable to learn.

The report that a boy in Amberson Valley had shot at the "gorilla" twice is most emphatically denied by people living in that section.

The *Chambersburg Public*

Opinion today reassured the timid folks living about Edenville and Cashtown, Franklin county, that so far as they were able to diagnose the "gorilla" scare in their territory there was absolutely "nothing to it."

A report, said to have come from Orrstown, was to the effect that the "gorilla" had broken into several smoke houses in that vicinity one night, eating part of a ham at one place and carrying off three hams from the other for "his" breakfast the next morning. The hotel at Orrstown has not had license for a number of years and we are unable to account for a story such as this coming from that pretty, little thriving village.

The story is told of a young man living in the "West End" of Shippensburg, who had always slept with the window of his bedroom wide open, but after hearing the "gorilla" story, closed it, procured a heavy nail and with a hammer drove it in solid above the sash. This young man is taking no chance of the "gorilla" reaching through the window and pulling him out of bed, and is to be commended for his "Safety First" principles.

One of the latest rumors is that the "gorilla" came to Shippensburg from somewhere near Harrisburg, on a Western Maryland freight train. It is said "he" jumped off the cars at the Peerless Table Company's plant and started for Newburg via Newcomertown and Middle Spring.

Some parents of the town think it would be a good thing to have a "gorilla" about all the time, as they have noted a very decided tendency amongst the children to hang close to the home fire-side in the evenings. They believe it would accomplish better results than a "curfew bell."

In conversation with a citizen of Shippensburg several days ago, he remarked that the present "gorilla" story recalled to his memory the "Gum Devil" scare with which Shippensburg was afflicted about 25 years ago. In those days when parents wanted their children in the home at night all that was necessary was to mention the "Gum Devil". It was a sure cure. He told of how, after being out at nights some times spending the evening with his "best girl," upon starting for home he would take the middle of the street and of how much easier and freely he breathed after he had arrived inside his home and the door was closed, shutting out the imaginary terrors that roamed outside.

Wood's Natural History describes a gorilla as follows: "The gorilla the most man-like of the apes, lives in the forests of Africa. It is shorter but broader than the average man, being about 5 ½ feet high and about 38 inches from shoulder to shoulder. The neck is short, the forehead retreating, the nose flat, the arms very long and strong, the jaws enormous with large canine teeth. The body is covered with iron-grey hair, while the hair on the head is reddish. Its favorite food is the wild sugar-cane and nuts. When attacked by hunters, it beats its breast with its large paws, gives terrible roars, and if not fatally wounded at once, flings itself on the hunter, crushing both the weapon and the man."

If you see an animal corresponding with the above description you may safely conclude that it is a gorilla and you should lose no time in reporting the fact to the State Police.[35]

◆

Several weeks ago a Snyder county newspaper correspondent, who needed the money, sent a special to the Philadelphia newspapers detailing the hair-raising experiences of several Snyder county farmers with a gorilla or ape-man which had escaped from a New York city zoo and made his way through the mountains to that vicinity. That story furnished a productive lead to several other fellows in different sections of the state who "lie about their neighbors for a living," and soon the gorilla was reported from these several different sections of the state. He appeared on four or five dollars worth around Patton and northern Cambria county with the result that various natives are now running into him everywhere.

It remained for a West Side citizen to land the ape-man close to home. This man approached Mayor Chase this morning and asked that vigilant guardian of the welfare and morals of the community what provision he had made to protect our citizens from a possible visit from the gorilla. The mayor said "Goshang it, I hain't never heard of him." Then the West Sider broke the news of the depredations of the hairy monster. He cited the numerous instances of the ape-man's appearance as given in the daily papers from time to time and then knocked the mayor stiff with a story that the huge gorilla had appeared last night at Wallaceton, that he had killed and half eaten a farmer's calf in a barn yard handy to the town, that help had been asked of the Wallaceton people and a posse raised by the blowing of the brickyard whistle. Fifty men started out to round up the beast but that Jim Berton, superintendent at the brick works, had run into him and the beast picked up a club and ran Jim half a mile before he succeeded in swatting him with the club. Two blows of the club was said to have stretched Jim on the ground and when assistance arrived the animal beat it through the red brush in the direction of Morrisdale.

The mayor's informant said Jim was being brought to the Clearfield Hospital on the 11:13 Pennsy train, but he didn't come, and therefore we are now satisfied some fellow filled our west side friend with sawdust; that the gorilla did not appear and that it is the same ape-man that has not appeared anywhere else of the many places mentioned in the state papers the past few weeks.[36]

———◆———

First it is the firebug, then the "poison pen" writer. Now comes the cheerful liar. A man representing himself as a resident of Reidmore called *The Courier* this morning to say that a "gorilla" had been seen in that locality last night and had been shot at and that it had eaten two pigs belonging to Isaac Mulnix. The informant said the alleged animal had been followed up Reidmore hollow well into the woods and that "everybody is afraid."

Inquiry of several persons in the locality developed that there had been no excitement of any kind; that no pigs had disappeared at the place mentioned, and that nobody had heard of a gorilla or any other animal.[37]

———◆———

PONDEROUS HOOF OF NEGRO GAVE GORILLA YARN START

Men Anxious To Frighten Trespassers Had Him Walk Barefoot In Snow — Heroic Spoof Had Desired Effect.

Cumberland, Md., Jan. 15. — The story of the "gorilla" that is supposed to have terrorized the mountainous district of Bedford county, Pennsylvania, not far north of the Mason Dixon Line, has come to light. While it would probably be an easy thing to secure a score of people who would declare under oath they had seen it and heard it or saw depredations it committed, it is now made known what really did happen. A vigilance committee had been formed and was armed to the teeth. Men stood guard all night long, watching for the gorilla to appear that they might riddle him with bullets.

This is the story: Two men engaged in lumber manufacturing just outside the limits of Claysburg had a large tract of timber on which were growing many small pine and spruce trees, which people of the community were accustomed to cut for Christmas trees without asking permission, thereby working considerable destruction.

These lumbermen worked out a plan to stop the stealing of trees. They had in their employ a negro who had enormous feet. There was snow on the ground and they had the negro take off his boots and walk about where the evergreen trees grew, making the imprint of immense feet in the snow.

This was enough. The persons who saw the track first may be running yet. At any rate, the alarm spread, and it had the effect desired — not a single tree was removed from that particular wood. Now the lumbermen are telling the story and laughing.[38]

———◆———

THOUGHT THEY SAW GORILLA

Wildest of Wild Rumors Has Reached Gettysburg.

One of the wildest of the many wild rumors that circulate throughout Adams county reached Gettysburg today. According to this unfounded report a huge gorilla was spied sitting on a rock near Mount Rock Wednesday afternoon. When the monstrous animal saw that it was discovered by some Mount Rock citizens it arose, stretched itself, and disappeared into a nearby wood, according to the report.

When told this story one Gettysburg citizen said, "It is evident that some of my Mount Rock friends are seeing more peculiar visions now than they did before the advent of the Eighteenth Amendment."[39]

———◆———

It is reported that a man who was cutting wood on a farm near Shippensburg, one day last week, imagined he saw the Gorilla looking over a pile of wood at him just as he quit work for the day. Those who know him state that he is a very fast runner, but on this occasion broke all records for speed. Upon reaching home he discovered he had jarred loose and lost every buckle on his arctics in his mad flight for a place of safety.[40]

◆

GORILLA STORY NO LONGER A MYTH

Residents of Idaville and Vicinity Conducted Chase Thursday Night.

That the story of a huge gorilla frightening the people of Adams county is not a myth but an actual fact is the emphatic statement of northern county residents who late Thursday night took part in a general chase in the vicinity of Idaville.

For several days reports believed to be entirely unfounded reached Gettysburg from northern county people stating that they had seen an animal believed to be a gorilla prowling about their property. At first these reports were discredited by the majority of people who heard them but now they are known to have originated from authentic sources.

Thursday afternoon and evening a general chase with the gorilla as the objective was conducted by the residents of Idaville and vicinity. The animal described by some as a gorilla and by others as a kangaroo was first seen at Snyder's hill between York Springs and Idaville where a number of men failed in a combined attempt to capture or shoot it. At 10 o'clock Thursday night about fifty men gathered on Pike hill near Idaville and again vainly tried to kill the elusive creature which escaped across the snow to Daniels' hill near the Adams-Cumberland county line.

The theory advanced for the animal is that it escaped from a circus train during a railroad wreck several months ago.

So far no damage by the animal has been done excepting the robbery of a smoke house attributed to it.[41]

◆

"GORILLA" WAS A MULE

Man Got Excited and Shot Neighbor's Beast of Burden.

Stories of a wandering gorilla caused the shooting of a mule when Abraham Lau, of Franklintown, York county mistook the animal for the much talked of wild beast. Saturday night Mr. Lau went to his back yard to bring a bucket of coal, says a news report from Franklintown, and saw what he thought was the "gorilla." He became alarmed and went to the house for his gun. He shot and badly injured his neighbor's mule.[42]

Latest report from the "gorilla" says that "he" was seen in Adams county and that hunters had gotten so close on his tracks there that "he" is now headed for Cumberland county again.[43]

SEE "GORILLA" AGAIN

Waynesboro Man On Way to Work Saw It.

The "gorilla" visions of which have been reported in this county, and which has furnished new stories from various sections of the state, has been seen in Waynesboro, it is said.

Harry Shindledecker, an employee of the trolley company in Waynesboro was on his way to work Wednesday morning and while passing the baseball grounds saw something he took to be the animal. He arrived at the car barn in an excited condition. He said the animal was about the height of a man.[44]

BRAVE MEN START OUT TO GET GORILLA

Waynesboro, Jan. 28. — When Henry Needy, of Rouzerville, started for town after supper Wednesday night his path was crossed by a great, black object which he believes was the gorilla that has been reported in sections of Franklin and Adams county recently.

Needy "beat it" for McCleaf's store, where, after listening to his story, a party which later totaled twenty-five brave men, started to comb the fields and dark spots in and near town. Several shots were fired by members of the party who "thought they saw something." Two of the shots took effect in the bodies of innocent dogs who were participating in the chase.

In the meantime a number of young single and married women who were visiting among their neighbors became excited and as the time of going home approached sent out S. O. S. calls for escorts. For an hour or two "seeing a lady home" became the prevailing duty of a number of Rouzerville's beau brummels'.

The "gorilla" is still at large.[45]

CHASE GORILLA TO MOUNTAINS

Posse of Rouzerville Citizens Make Futile Attempt to Kill Animal.

VILLAGE WAS IN UPROAR

Marksmen Form Line of Attack But Gorilla Makes Escape. Was Seen at Monterey Golf Links.

"Gorilla" warfare which was started last week in the vicinity of Idaville when Adams county residents, well armed, pursued what is believed to be an animal that escaped from a circus car when it wrecked, not long ago, was renewed by citizens of Rouzerville Wednesday night when an armed posse scoured the Blue Ridge slopes in the hope of getting a shot at the beast.

The animal was discovered in an alley just as dusk was falling on the village. The word was quickly spread and the members of the Rouzerville deer camp and every one else that had a rifle soon turned out for the hunt. After the mobilization of marksmen was completed, the attackers in battle formation started up the mountain.

Gorilla Chased Out

They barely had gotten underway when the animal was chased out. Although a number of shots were fired the chimpanzee kept on bounding toward the thicker brush of the slope. It was then that an elaborate campaign was decided on and a messenger was sent for reinforcements. The firing on the mountain was heard in the village and the town was soon in an uproar. It was decided to form a great circle around the foothill where the animal was last seen. Deployed in this fashion the grizzled hunters and young marksmen moved into the woodland.

Dog Pays Penalty

They scoured the mountain slope halfway to Pen Mar but found no trace of the gorilla. A black dog running through the underbrush paid the death penalty when an excited hunter mistook it for the ape.

When the hunters returned from the mountains, reports say, the town was in a turmoil — the animal had been seen there while the hunt was on. Young women who happened to be on the streets when the "panic" started were afraid to go home and escorts had to be provided.

Since the Rouzerville affair, the gorilla has been seen at

Monterey by two young men who were on their way home from a party. As they neared the Monterey golf links, they saw what they thought was a man approaching on all fours. When they called the animal rose on its hind legs and came toward them making gurgling sounds. The young men did not investigate any further.[46]

SAW GORILLA IN DAYLIGHT

Animal Has Haunt In Mountain according To Reports.

The big gorilla, which has been wandering in the mountains of southern Pennsylvania for some weeks, has turned up again near Pen Mar, according to reports from that section.

The big ape was seen by John Simmons, who resides between Pen Mar and Rouzerville, Saturday afternoon, while the light of the sun was so bright it could leave no doubt upon the mind or vision. Simmons was going through a field near his home, when he saw a strange, unlikely object, which he at once connected with the "gorilla", from descriptions he had read in the newspapers.

At the time he saw the strange animal, Simmons was not armed and he was not in the mood to enter combat with the gorilla.[47]

GORILLA ECHOES

MAITLAND, Pa., Feb. 15. — Mrs. S. E. Krepps was terribly frightened today when she saw what she believed to be the far famed gorilla of Snyder county in a dark corner of the cellar. The object, covered with hair, which she could just distinguish in the darkness, appeared to groan and when in its sleep and calling her husband who procured the gun they went to the cellar only to find it was a beef hide the husband placed there at the week end.[48]

Q. How many gorillas are in captivity in the United States?

A. So far as we are able to ascertain, there are no gorillas in captivity in the United States at the present time. The New York zoo did have one for a number of months, but it died some time ago.[49]

THE BAD GORILLA WAS A RACCOON

The gorilla story that swept through the central part of the state several months ago, when it was reported that a gorilla had escaped from a traveling show, is now known to have been a genuine hoax.

A bear trap, originally set for the gorilla and said to have been carried away by the animal, was found Wednesday at the foot of the Seven Mountains on the farm of Will John Henry, who had set the trap. In the confines of the jaws of the bear trap was a raccoon. The animal was nothing but skin and bones from the effects of the torture suffered during the many weeks it had dragged the trap through the mountains. The animal was given its liberty and dragged itself off into the woods.[50]

TOWN RESIDENTS SEE "GORILLA"

Strange Beast Shot at by York Street Citizen. Found Footprints, Too.

It's in. again.

After having passed out of the limelight several months ago, the well known "gorilla" is back. It was in Gettysburg several nights ago, according to information from well informed circles.

It was not only seen but shot at.

Whether or not it was wounded is not known, but it departed hurriedly from lower York street in the direction of Biglerville.

Not long ago a woman residing on York street saw a strange object about four feet high moving along the fence in rear of her house, it is said, and being alone, she rushed to the place next door seeking help. The man of the house secured a shotgun. He too saw the beast. He fired. The gorilla dropped to the ground.

Thinking he had bagged his game the gunner went toward the fallen animal. When only a few feet away the beast jumped to its hind legs and chased the man into the house, residents of that part of town declare. Those who ventured to look out say the animal disappeared in the direction of Biglerville. In fact, they declare an examination of the ground in a field nearby revealed foot prints of a strange beast.

A number of York street residents have oiled shotguns long obscured and a second visit by the beast to that part of town would probably result fatally for it. Others believe the animal by this time has returned to the fastnesses of the mountains.[51]

◆

GORILLA SPIED ALONG HIGHWAY

Elusive Animal Seen Squatting Near Fort Louden in The Moonlight.

Fleeter of foot than Paddock the California sprinter, more strongly built for endurance than Jack Dempsey, the heavyweight champion, and far more elusive than a bootlegger to would be captors is the one and only Gorilla.

Miles are nothing in the life of this animal whose fame has spread throughout Pennsylvania and northern Maryland. One night he is seen cavorting over the hillsides between York Springs and Gardners in northern Adams county. The next night he looms up in Biglerville, then Gettysburg and ere a week flits by he is seen in the hills of Franklin county or Maryland. What an asset to a football coach planning for a successful season would be this never weary animal who flits from mountain top to mountain.

Friday night he was seen again.

Just a short time ago a York street resident in Gettysburg fired a load of shot at the rapidly disappearing figure of this noted beast. Since leaving here in the direction of Biglerville the gorilla evidently has made a semi-circular jaunt for he was seen Friday night near Fort Louden.

While coming home from Pittsburgh where he attended a meeting of Lincoln Highway officials, Howard C. Mitinger, of Gettysburg, saw the gorilla sitting on a stump along the highway a short distance west of Fort Louden. "He was plainly discernible in the moonlight," said the secretary.

To corroborate his statements Mr. Mitinger has his sister-in-law Mrs. George Ramsey, of Huntington; her daughter, Miss Jean Ramsey; and Robert Mathias, steward of the Hoffman hotel, who were with him at the time.[52]

WHO LEFT THE DOOR OPEN?

Only Original Gorilla Seen In County Again.

The original Adams county gorilla which occasionally flits across the mountains into Franklin county is in the vicinity of Fairfield if reports from that section are to be believed.

Sunday evening while driving along the Fairfield road Ray Weikert saw the animal plainly as it crossed the road not many feet in front of his horse, according to reports from that region. Not only did the young man see the beast, but the horse as well, and it was with difficulty it was kept from running away. The animal crossed the road leisurely, walking on its hind legs, climbed the fence and disappeared in the underbrush. It was described as being about five feet tall.[53]

♦

Stories that a "wild man" has been making his home along the rocky ledge near Nescopeck have been confirmed by Kingsley Williams and Mr. Henninger, of Nescopeck, who, while hunting, saw the strange man. It was thought that the stranger was an escaped prisoner, but this has proved false.[54]

♦

[1] *The Evening News* (Wilkes-Barre, PA) January 2, 1920.

[2] *Pittsburgh Daily Post* (Pittsburgh, PA) August 21, 1920.
Here begins a wave of "gorilla" sightings which sweep across Pennsylvania in the early 1920s.

[3] *The Pittsburgh Press* (Pittsburgh, PA) August 21, 1920.

[4] *The Pittsburgh Press* (Pittsburgh, PA) August 22, 1920.

[5] Illustration from *New Castle News* (New Castle, PA) October 18, 1920.

[6] *Pittsburgh Post-Gazette* (Pittsburgh, PA) August 22, 1920.

[7] *Pittsburgh Daily Post* (Pittsburgh, PA) August 23, 1920.

[8] *The Pittsburgh Press* (Pittsburgh, PA) August 23, 1920.

[9] *New Castle News* (New Castle, PA) August 24, 1920.

[10] *The Pittsburgh Press* (Pittsburgh, PA) August 25, 1920.

[11] *The Pittsburgh Press* (Pittsburgh, PA) August 26, 1920.

[12] *The Daily Republican* (Monogahela, PA) September 11, 1920.

[13] *The Daily Notes* (Canonsburg, PA) September 25, 1920.

[14] *The Evening News* (Harrisburg, PA) December 11, 1920.
Young Boilig is assaulted by a "gorilla" and left in critical condition. The names (first and last) change slightly, but presumably there was only one "gorilla" attack around this time and place.

[15] *Harrisburg Telegraph* (Harrisburg, PA) December 14, 1920.

[16] *Evening Report* (Lebanon, PA) December 14, 1920.
Here we get a little more information and we find out for the first time that the "gorilla" was injured by the young Boling weeks before the attack. Some modern reports point to bigfoot creatures having a sort of "culture of revenge" - if someone hurts them, the creatures will seek to hurt them back - to the point of following people home at times, and waiting for an opportune moment to take their revenge.

[17] *The Evening News* (Wilkes-Barre, PA) December 14, 1920.

More details about the Boilig/Boling/Bolling incident. The quote from the victim "the big animal more than feet high" is not a mistake on my part - this is how it was printed in the paper.

[18] *The Evening News* (Harrisburg, PA) December 14, 1920.

Here we get some new and different details on the case. It is hard to say which reporter, if any, got the story right. We do, at least, get a height from the attack victim here - over 7 feet! As a note - the tallest African gorilla on record is 6'4".

[19] *Altoona Tribune* (Altoona, PA) December 15, 1920.

Another differing account of the "gorilla" attack in Snyder county. While the details surrounding the attack seem to shift from paper to paper, the attack itself and the size of the creature remain consistent.

[20] *Mount Carmel Item* (Mount Carmel, PA) December 15, 1920.

[21] *Mount Carmel Item* (Mount Carmel, PA) December 18, 1920.

[22] *The Pittsburgh Press* (Pittsburgh, PA) December 18, 1920.

It seems the sightings were so shocking, rare, and strange, that it never occurred to people at the time that there may be more than one creature. With the number of "gorilla" reports throughout Pennsylvania in the 1920s it seems likely there were multiple creatures.

[23] *Altoona Tribune* (Altoona, PA) December 20, 1920.

[24] *Altoona Tribune* (Altoona, PA) December 20, 1920.

[25] *Altoona Tribune* (Altoona, PA) December 21, 1920.

This seems to be a good time to remind the reader that, though the author of this report seems to be convinced this creature is an escaped African gorilla, we are talking about December in Pennsylvania - and a long time from when and where the animal supposedly escaped. It is extremely doubtful an escaped African gorilla could survive in the wilds of Pennsylvania, in the cold months, subsisting on a diet of strange and unfamiliar foods. Not to mention the reported size of the creature(s) in question puts them outside the height of even the tallest African gorillas. A reminder too that "bigfoot", "sasquatch", and similar terms simply were not in the vocabulary of people at this time. The description and behavior of this creature or creatures is completely consistent with bigfoot reports.

[26] *Altoona Tribune* (Altoona, PA) December 21, 1920.

[27] *Altoona Tribune* (Altoona, PA) December 21, 1920.
How much in common these "gorilla" reports have with modern bigfoot accounts! We read of footprints, livestock killings, roadside sightings - even a man with a megaphone whose calls are answered back! Even the most casual bigfoot enthusiast has likely seen the various television shows where people make their own calls or broadcast recordings of other recordings through loudspeakers (this is known as "call blasting").

[28] *Pittsburgh Daily Post* (Pittsburgh, PA) December 21, 1920.

[29] *Altoona Tribune* (Altoona, PA) December 22, 1920.

[30] *Altoona Tribune* (Altoona, PA) December 22, 1920.

[31] *Altoona Tribune* (Altoona, PA) December 22, 1920.

[32] *Altoona Tribune* (Altoona, PA) December 27, 1920.

[33] *Altoona Tribune* (Altoona, PA) December 28, 1920.

[34] *Altoona Tribune* (Altoona, PA) December 29, 1920.

[35] *The Chronicle* (Shippensburg, PA) January 13, 1921.

[36] *The Progress* (Clearfield, PA) January 14, 1921.
I have taken to saying lately that being a skeptic in regards to things paranormal or cryptozoological in nature is the easiest thing in the world. You simply claim that every witness is either drunk, stoned, stupid, or crazy; every reporter who tells only what witnesses saw is trying to make a buck on sensationalism; every film or photo is a fake or inconclusive; etc. It's an easy formula, and one that has been around for a long, long time as evidenced by this reporter, and some of the others above. Still, there is some interesting information within this article about another possible bigfoot attack - which seems to be consistent with the creature(s) roaming about Pennsylvania at this time - and another attack on livestock.

[37] *The Daily Courier* (Connellsville, PA) January 15, 1921.

[38] *The Baltimore Sun* (Baltimore, MD) January 16, 1921.
Besides the sad and obvious racism shown in this article, this

"solution" to the gorilla sightings is absolutely ridiculous. How could a few footprints on one property account for all of the sightings? This calls to mind the claims of Ray Wallace and family that he hoaxed the very footprints found in California in the 1950s which led to the name "bigfoot" - and that he had created many, many other sets of bigfoot prints in California and the Northwest - using big fake wooden feet. Some papers reported "Bigfoot is dead" when Ray Wallace died - as if one man and a set of wooden feet could account for every track, every sighting, and every other bit of evidence ever found. Bigfoot sightings, footprints, and other associated evidence continued after Ray Wallace died - just as the "gorilla" reports continue after this article.

[39] *The Gettysburg Times* (Gettysburg, PA) January 20, 1921.

[40] *The Chronicle* (Shippensburg, PA) January 20, 1921.

[41] *The Gettysburg Times* (Gettysburg, PA) January 21, 1921.

[42] *The Gettysburg Times* (Gettysburg, PA) January 25, 1921.

[43] *The Chronicle* (Shippensburg, PA) January 27, 1921.

[44] *The Gettysburg Times* (Gettysburg, PA) January 27, 1921.

[45] *Harrisburg Telegraph* (Harrisburg, PA) January 28, 1921.

[46] *The Gettysburg Times* (Gettysburg, PA) January 28, 1921.
Poor mules and dogs seem to be getting the worst of these "gorilla" hunts!

[47] *The Gettysburg Times* (Gettysburg, PA) February 1, 1921.

[48] *Altoona Tribune* (Altoona, PA) February 16, 1921.

[49] *New Castle Herald* (New Castle, PA) March 17, 1921.
This was an interesting little "Q & A" I found from the time of the "gorilla" sightings in Pennsylvania. While this was not tied directly to the sightings in question, it does show how rare African gorillas were, even in captivity, in the United States at this time. This casts the "escaped gorilla" hypothesis even further into doubt.

[50] *Mount Carmel Item* (Mount Carmel, PA) March 24, 1921.
It takes great leaps of logic to make this raccoon story "work" as a solution to the "gorilla" sightings! The trap was set in an effort to catch

the "gorilla" - so this raccoon would have had to make his way through Pennsylvania before *and* after its capture in the bear trap (as there are sightings yet to come). How this one raccoon "proves" the sightings are all a hoax is beyond my reasoning. Not to mention the bizarre idea that *anyone* could confuse a raccoon with a "gorilla" - let alone all of the witnesses noted here.

[51] *The Gettysburg Times* (Gettysburg, PA) August 9, 1921.

This is the famous "Gettysburg Gorilla" shooting story. At only four feet, this creature seems considerably smaller than the "gigantic gorillas" reported previously, leading me to believe there was more than one "gorilla" prowling about Pennsylvania.

[52] *The Gettysburg Times* (Gettysburg, PA) August 13, 1921.

[53] *The Gettysburg Times* (Gettysburg, PA) August 24, 1921.

[54] *Pittston Gazette* (Pittston, PA) November 18, 1921.

APPENDIX I

A NEARBY GORILLA REPORT

'WILD GORILLA' IN WOODS STIRS 6 NEARBY TOWNS

Armed Posse Searching Region Around Joppa For Grizzly Animal.

RESIDENTS ALL CARRY GUNS

One Party of Hunters Reports Seeing Quadruped Fleeing Among the Trees.

Reports of a "great hairy animal that walks like a man" lurking in the woods terrorized the more timorous residents of the little settlements of Wilna, Abingdon, Joppa, Edgewood, Magnolia, and Bradshaw last night, led to the formation of armed posses to hunt the beast and to the carrying of shotguns by most persons who found it necessary to be outdoors.

The telephone operator at Wilna was instructed to call up all numbers on the exchange and warn them that the animal, which most persons said looked like a gorilla, was reported at large. At Abingdon an armed posse of 16 to 20 men was organized. Men stood around in the general stores of several settlements with shotguns slung across their arms.

Six Say They Saw Beast.

Six persons declared

positively they had seen the hairy beast. None, however, was able to describe it accurately. They reported that in spite of its size and grizzly appearance it appeared to be as timorous as a gazelle and elusive as a will-o'-the-wisp.

The first who said she saw the animal was Mrs. Joseph Mosedale, who lives about a half-mile from Abingdon. Early in the morning, she said, she left her home and saw the hairy creature coming directly toward her. She screamed and fled back into the house. The animal, she said, also turned when she shouted and made off into the woods.

At noon Harry and Herbery Mosedale, sons of Mrs. Mosedale, said they saw the animal running through the woods. In the afternoon George Reynolds, a merchant in the vicinity; Elmer Jauresk and a negro, Philip Cromwell armed themselves with shotguns and beat through the woods. Reynolds on his return declared the party had caught a fleeting glimpse of the animal, but that it plunged into a thicket before he or any of the others could fire.

Talk of Asking Soldiers Heard.

The report spread quickly. Railroad employees spread it all along the line and by night the entire section was agog with the tales of the strange beast. Men armed themselves and the posse was organized. The advisability of calling upon the commandment at the Edgewood Arsenal for a detachment of soldiers to join the hunt was discussed. Major Meredith, the officer in charge, however, said no such call was made upon him.

Various explanations were offered around the stoves in the corner groceries as the men gravely discussed the danger they had been told threatened. Some held tenaciously to the theory that it was an escaped animal from a circus that exhibited at Havre de Grace a week ago, Others blamed it all on the particularly bad brands of "hootch" that have been reaching the section within the last few weeks.[1]

[1] *The Baltimore Sun* (Baltimore, MD) October 29, 1921.

The "gorilla" - if it is indeed just one animal - seems to have made its way from central Pennsylvania down through Adams County and across into northern Maryland. Note that this report falls two months after the last "Gettysburg Gorilla" report.

APPENDIX II

MYSTERY LIGHTS

Frightened to Death. — A young lady, Miss Stewart, of Cumberland county, Pa., was so badly scared a few weeks ago by meeting a will-o'the-wisp that she was taken ill on reaching home, and in a short time afterward died from the effects of the prostration of her nervous system, superintended by the fright.[1]

◆

A Strange Light. — A mysterious light, mistaken for a burning ship, was noticed on Lake Erie a week or so ago. The light has made its appearance generally, if not always, in the fall of the year, and usually in the month of November, and almost always during or immediately after a heavy blow from the southwest. A correspondent says: "I am told that this light was seen by mariners on the lake as long as fifty years ago, but I am not aware that it has ever been made the subject of philosophical speculation. The only theory I have is, that the shifting of the sands caused by the continued and heavy winds of the autumn, has opened some crevices or seams in the rock of the lake-bottom through which gas escapes, and that this gas, owing to some peculiar condition of the atmosphere with which it comes in contact, becomes luminous, or, perhaps, ignited and burning with a positive flame. That there are what are styled "gas springs" in the water all along this portion of the lake shore is a well known fact, and that a highly inflammable gas in large quantities exists at a comparatively shallow depth on the shore, has been proved by the boring of wells at different points.[2]

───────◆───────

FIERY BALLS. — We are informed that several persons in the country, near town, report having seen on Saturday night last, two large fiery balls descending from the sky, and falling to the ground in a field some distance from them.[3]

───────◆───────

A BERKS COUNTY STORY.

A Strange Light at Midnight Causes a Runaway — One Young Lady Dragged to Death, Another Dangerously Hurt and a Boy Injured — The Victim's Mother at the Point of Death.

Womelsdorf correspondent writes: On Saturday evening Miss Kate Leininger, daughter of Gorge Leininger, a beautiful young lady eighteen years of age, accompanied by a lady friend, Miss Ada Hoffman, only daughter of Franklin Hoffman, and a young son of Mr. Hoffman, all from Newmanstown, Lebanon county, started away from home in a buggy in the best of health and spirits to visit the ladies' fair now in progress in Schaefferstown, Lebanon county. The three arrived safely at the fair and spent the evening very joyfully, especially the ladies. At nearly twelve o'clock they started home, the night being very dark and stormy, making driving rather difficult. When the parties had come within about a mile east of Schaefferstown, a light appeared before the horse, which scared the ladies badly as well as the young boy. The place has been for many years known as "the spook place," no doubt the light being what is known as Will-o'-the-wisp or Jack of the Lantern. The horse took fright and commenced to run off at a rapid rate, and the young boy, who is about fourteen years of age, insists upon and says that he was sure that something had jumped on the horses back, which still increased the speed of the animal and the fright of the ladies. When they reached a bridge spanning the Mill Creek, about three quarters of a mile west of Newmanstown, the horse ran upon a stone heap and fell, breaking the shafts, which then made the horse kick, when the young boy jumped out of the buggy, taking the lines along. Miss Hoffman, being a stout, robust and beautiful young lady, told her companion, Miss Leininger to jump out also, when Miss Leininger tried to persuade her not to jump at the same time taking hold of her clothing. Miss Hoffman, however, jumped and was caught in the wheels, and was whirled around the wheel several times, when she was extricated from her perilous position. Miss Leininger, who was still sitting in the buggy, then also jumped out and was caught with one foot in the half-moon at the shafts and with the other leg at the axle, when she was so firmly wedged into the left front wheel that she could not extricate herself, and the wheel was entirely locked, and in that fearful position she was dragged over half a mile with her head down, going over the rough and stony road, making a drag into the street same as if a heavy log had been dragged. The wheel had the appearance as though it had been washed in blood. Franklin Hoffman, father of Ada Hoffman, was sitting up and waiting for his children to come home. At half-past one o'clock he heard a horse and buggy pass his house and when he went out to look he saw the horse going past only on a walk. Not knowing that it was his horse, the night being very dark, he went into his house again. In a few minutes his children came running and informed him of the sad news, when Mr. Hoffman ran after the horse and stopped him. Mrs. Clara Noll, still being up and waiting for her husband, who had also been to Schaefferstown, heard the noise and ran out, when she saw that Miss Leininger was still wedged into the wheel. She pulled her out, which was all she could do, Mr. Hoffman holding the horse, which seemed to be greatly excited. Very soon a large crowd appeared on the spot and Dr. Seth Smith was summoned, who called to his assistance Dr. Raudenbush, of Adamstown, Lancaster county, who had been on a visit to friends in Newmanstown. After a careful examination of Miss Leininger, they found that life had been extinct before the horse had been caught. She had been hurt and mangled terribly, her whole face and even her whole body was one mass of blood and bruises.

Miss Hoffman is lying in bed and is delirious all the time, getting violent spasms, calling and begging for her dear, dear friend. She is considered dangerously hurt and may not survive her injuries.

The young boy escaped with a few slight bruises.

Miss Leininger was an accomplished young lady and was very highly spoken of in her neighborhood. Her loss is felt deeply among her many friends. She will be buried tomorrow (Tuesday) morning at Newmanstown church.

The parents of both families have sympathies of the entire neighborhood.

Mrs. Leininger can hardly survive the terrible shock, as she is a very weak woman. She has been lying in hysterics all the time since her daughter has been brought home.[4]

— Now for a ghost story: One evening recently Messrs Albert and Park Grove were coming up the R. R. track to Tionesta from president, and when near Hunter's Station they noticed a light, apparently on the track, about forty rods ahead of them. As it appeared to grow larger, one of the gentlemen remarked that it must be coming toward them rapidly, as it was continually growing larger. So they stepped off the track and took the wagon road until they were opposite the light, which appeared about a foot and a half in diameter. Finally Park remarked that he wished it would come up towards them, when lo! the light made a break for them, and approached within about a rod of them, and about ten feet in the air. Park heaved a stone at the light, and it moved off in nearly the same direction from which it came. The light was still there when they left, and they are unable to explain the phenomenon. It was undoubtably a will-o'-the-wisp, which Esq. Irwin explains on chemical principles.[5]

A Ghost Scare in Lebanon.

On a lot one square north of the Hartman House, Lebanon, is a lot in which the ground is low and marshy, and over this the singular spectacle of an *ignis fatuus*, or "jack-a-lantern," has been noticed several nights recently, causing considerable uproar. Persons passing that way have been scared badly by this strange moving light, and the place has got the reputation of being haunted. A bulletin board has been erected near by on which is written "Beware of Ghosts!" The Lebanon *Daily Times* says that the other night a watchman passing near that place was so frightened that his hair stood straight as the quills of a porcupine, and he declared that he heard some queer noises in the lot. On Thursday night at 11 o'clock several ladies and gentlemen returning from a sociable noticed the strange but brilliant *ignis fatuus* moving about near the pavement. The heroic young men at once took to their heels and disappeared, leaving the frightened ladies to their fate. Two of them screamed at the top of their voices and fainted on the spot. A policeman came to the rescue and promptly blew his whistle, which brought along two more officers, and they succeeded in quieting the frightened females, convincing them that the light was no ghost, but only a harmless "will-o'the-wisp," and then escorted them home.[6]

◆

A mysterious light seen at night on a particular grave in the Lutheran cemetery in Bloomfield excites an uncommon interest in that community.[7]

◆

On last Friday night a mysterious light was seen high up on Shade mountain north of this place, and on Saturday night about 8 o'clock a light was seen high on the mountain side, seemingly, just west of Macedonia Gap. The light appeared like the bright light of a lantern or torch.[8]

◆

HUMMELSTOWN has a real "will o' the wisp." A "righty" "jack o' the lantern," as the children would say. It has been in the possession of Hummelstown for nearly a score of years. Gossip saw the mysterious light last night. It is opposite the P. & R. station and sticks to the bluff overhanging the Swatara creek and strangers always make an effort to see it.[9]

PHANTOMS OF FIRE.

Remarkable Electric Phenomena at Undercliff, Out the P. & W.

A HILL SEEMS TO BE CHARGED.

It Robs the Clouds of Lighting and Terrifies the People.

SCENES DURING THUNDER STORMS

A hillside extracting lightning from the sky is by no means a common spectacle. But it is witnessed quite frequently by people living just a short distance from Pittsburgh. It has been especially noticeable during the recent electric storms.

During storms, when the atmosphere and clouds are charged with electricity, showers of fire have been seen to issue from the sky and, descending upon this magic mount, form into various colored blazes and go dancing along the ground like Wills-of-the-Wisp. Then suddenly they sink into the earth and are gone. The phenomenon is of such frequent occurrence that the people residing near the mount have ceased to wonder at it.

"It has never done us no harm," said one old man, "and so we never pay any attention to it no more."

Almost in Sight of Pittsburg.

About six miles from Pittsburgh, on the Pittsburgh and Western Railroad, is a picturesque little place called Undercliff. It is just beyond the first tunnel. Immediately after emerging from the tunnel, the railroad winds along a rocky hillside which slants down into a pretty little valley. Just above the railroad track is a ledge of jagged rocks, which extend for some distance, suggesting the appropriate name which the place bears — Undercliff.

Near the center of this ledge the fiery phenomena occur. Just opposite the ledge, across the valley, another hillside rises with graceful slope, and here live the people who can tell thrilling tales of fiery storm phantoms which they have seen.

An old farmer. Daniel Baldwin, says it is a very common sight during storms to see balls of fire playing about among the underbrush and among the rocks across the valley. He has sat at his window many a time, he said, and watched them flitting about on the hillside and then disappear mysteriously into the ground. On one occasion, after an unusually violent atmospheric commotion, as many as a dozen or 15 fireballs were seen gamboling together. They were of various sizes and colors and made a very pretty display.

A Danger Signal on the Track.

Lawrence Smith, an ex-engineer of the Pittsburgh and Western Railroad, tells the following story:

"One stormy night several years ago my fireman and I witnessed an amazing sight near Undercliff. We were hauling a heavy freight from the west and had just rounded the sharp curve at Glenshaw, when a brilliant red light suddenly appeared on the track ahead of us. I took it for a danger signal and whistled 'down brakes' immediately. Being on the down grade the brakes were of little use and the train went thundering along the valley. As we neared the light we were surprised to find that it was acting in a very peculiar manner. It was describing circles and all kinds of figures in the air. Then all of a sudden it broke up into two lights, both of which lingered in the air for a moment and then mysteriously united again into a single light.

"But the most puzzling thing about the light was its location. It remained always the same distance ahead of us after we had come within about 40 yards of it, now bounding over the ties like a rubber ball, now hanging suspended in the air, and now sailing along the track like a bird. The mysterious light kept up this maneuvering until just a few feet from the tunnel, when it suddenly disappeared. The strange light must have followed along in front of our engine for half a mile or more."

Engulfed in a Sea of Fire.

An old farmer of that region, who is now dead, used to entertain his children in the evenings with stories of the Undercliff fire balls. One day while he was at work in a field above the cliff a heavy storm came up. The lightning became so frequent and threatening that he unhitched the horses from the plow and started down the winding road to the valley below. He had not proceeded far when the storm burst upon him with terrific fury. The lightning flashes seemed to be continuous and the man blinded by the glare imagined he was in the midst of a sea of fire. Spluttering balls of fire danced around him, played in the underbrush and went frisking about like rockets and roman candles in a pyrotechnic display. The fire finally all disappeared leaving the man and horses untouched.

Attracted by Cannon Balls.

An explanation of the phenomenon given by the country people is that the lightning is attracted to the place by a great mass of cannon balls which lie embedded in the hillside. Their theory is based upon the report that during the Civil War the valley at Undercliff was used as a testing ground for the cannons made in Pittsburgh foundries.

The cannon were stationed on the slope opposite the ledge and directed toward a target located at the base of the hillside. This, report would have it, and by the way it has many supporters, that so many cannon were made and consequently so many shots fired that the hill is fairly lined with iron cannon balls. The electrical phenomena is therefore simply a sequence.

But there is another explanation which, though not so wonderful as the former, is no doubt correct. It is that a vein of magnetic iron ore runs through the hill.[10]

---◆---

REYMEYER'S VALLEY JOTTINGS

Did you see the northern lights on Saturday night last, and can you tell us what caused them?[11]

---◆---

Keller's Church, over in Bedminster, has a sensation, it being asserted by some that the homestead of T. V. Kelly is haunted. People claim to have frequently seen a mysterious light wandering about the place at all hours of the night. The circumstance has created considerable talk in the neighborhood.[12]

---◆---

A MYSTERIOUS TRAVELING LIGHT.

— For years and years there has been seen periodically on the northern side of the Lehigh mountain, in western Salisbury, near Emaus, a mysterious light, it usually moving along from place to place. It appears at different times of the year, and whenever it makes itself visible causes much speculation and comment. One evening last week it again appeared above the Hinkle farm, showing up as bright and brilliant as an electric arc light. It after remaining stationary for a time moved along the mountain range to near Mountainville, and in its progress was seen by numerous people and gazed at in in wonderment by reason of being unable to account for it. On the front porch of farmer John Ohl the reflection cast off by it was so bright and brilliant that fine print could be read. It is quite unlike the common ignis fatuus or meteor light that sometimes appears in the night over marshy places and travels along roadways and across fields, occasionally scaring people out of their wits. The latter lights make themselves visible quite frequently, and are supposed to be occasioned by the decomposition of animal or vegetable substances, or by some inflammable gas. They are commonly called "Will-o'the wisp" or "Jack-with-a-lantern" lights. The Salisbury movable light is however of quite a different character — a sort of mysterious "What-Is-It" that nobody seems to be able to account for.

Many of the superstitious people of this section in which the light appears believe it to be the lantern of a traveling spook, and that a pile of money is buried somewhere along the mountain which the hobgoblin is guarding. The latter belief is quite ridiculous. We have never heard of any buccaneers coming so far inland to bury their treasure, and people in these parts have never had either money to bury or burn.[13]

PARK LIGHT. — Our suggestion that the mysterious light seen in the Park might be on the observatory at Lemon Hill is confirmed by a correspondent, who reports that he has frequently observed its resemblance to a star till it began to move.[14]

Swatara Astronomers Refuse to Admit That It's a Star.

JONESTOWN, May 15. — Throngs of people have nightly watched the mysterious light in the western sky, supposed to be an electric balloon sent up over Altoona by Mr. Edison in line with a proposed pyrotechnic entertainment or vaudeville novelty to which the sage is supposed to be giving his great brain. The residents of the northern section refuse to believe that the eccentric luminary is a star. It doesn't act like one, and no local astronomer has been found to say that it does.[15]

A MYSTERIOUS LIGHT

A mysterious light travels nightly over a portion of the Lofty mountain. It is as large as an arc light and appears at a regular time every night. Railroad men and others are much agitated over the appearance of the strange light. It was first seen near Malone's along the Delano mountain a few months ago.[16]

———————◆———————

Freeland. — Stockton, a mining town two miles south of this place, is greatly agitated over a mysterious light that hovers over the spot on the Ebervale mountain where the body of a woman was found in a barrel two years ago so charred that she was never identified.[17]

———————◆———————

MYSTERIOUS LIGHT AT NEWPORT.

A mysterious light on this side of the Newport bridge is attracting widespread attention. The watchman at the bridge and residents of Newport claim that the light has been seen for almost a year, but they have not been able to reach any definite conclusion regarding it. West Pittsburghers have just discovered it, however, and delegations have been visiting the place nightly. Spooks, ghosts, swamp light and many other theories have been advanced, but none seems to fit the case.[18]

———————◆———————

There are so many accounts of mystery lights in various forms - will-o-the-wisps, UFOs, etc - being associated with bigfoot sightings that I can't help but feel they are in some way connected. I cannot tell the reader exactly what the connection is, however. I do not believe bigfoot creatures are riding in UFOs or being dropped here by space aliens, but I do believe strange lights seem to often be seen in roughly the same time and place as bigfoot creatures. For this reason I have included in this section some reports of mystery lights I found while researching the other reports in this volume.

[1] *Gettysburg Compiler* (Gettysburg, PA) February 27, 1860.

[2] *Harrisburg Telegraph* (Harrisburg, PA) November 29, 1867.

[3] *The York Daily* (York, PA) May 16, 1872.

I have taken several modern reports of similar phenomena from the countryside around York - most notably the spooklights of Seven Valleys, as described in my book, *Beyond the Seventh Gate*.

[4] *The Pittsburgh Commercial* (Pittsburg, PA) June 21, 1876.

A tragic tale - but one wonders what the "something" was that jumped upon the horse's back. It is interesting that it is noted as a "something" and not a *someone*.

[5] *The Forest Republican* (Tionesta, PA) July 4, 1877.

[6] *Reading Times* (Reading, PA) December 12, 1881.

[7] *Juniata Sentinel and Republican* (Mifflintown, PA) November 17, 1886.

[8] *Juniata Sentinel and Republican* (Mifflintown, PA) November 24, 1886.

[9] *Harrisburg Telegraph* (Harrisburg, PA) May 17, 1889.

[10] *Pittsburgh Dispatch* (Pittsburgh, PA) June 31, 1892.

[11] *The York Daily* (York, PA) July 21, 1892.

[12] *The Central News* (Perkasie, PA) August 18, 1892.

[13] *The Allentown Democrat* (Allentown, PA) October 14, 1896.

[14] *The Philadelphia Inquirer* (Philadelphia, PA) September 24, 1897.

[15] *Lebanon Courier and Semi-Weekly Report* (Lebanon, PA) May 19, 1908.

[16] *Mount Carmel Item* (Mount Carmel, PA) December 1, 1908.

[17] *Harrisburg Telegraph* (Harrisburg, PA) January 15, 1909.

[18] *New Castle News* (New Castle, PA) January 24, 1919.

APPENDIX III

SOME OTHER STRANGE CREATURES IN PENNSYLVANIA

A What-Is-It.

Quite a large searching party has been organized in Berks County, Pa., for the purpose of scouring Muhlenberg and Ruscombmanor townships to hunt up and capture, if possible, one of the strangest looking beasts ever heard of within the borders of the county. What gives emphasis to the sincerity of the people engaged is the fact that responsible and reliable parties were first to report having seen the so-called monster. A son of Prison Inspector Schmehl was first to bring the intelligence to Topton Station. O. H. Hinnershitz, proprietor of the leading hotel there, and a number of others went in pursuit of what Schmehl described. The monster had been reported on previous occasions, and when Mr. Schmehl saw it it was lying near a gate entrance to a field through which he was driving a lot of cattle. The "what-is-it" is represented to be about four feet tall, long arms, with but two talon-like fingers on each paw: feet without toes, furrows on its head, body smooth and naked, quite yellow, looks as if it had been wallowing in clay. Jared Rissmiller heard of the animal. It had run up towards Schmehl with extended paws, and then darted into a corn field and was lost to view. The two men then went in search, and discovered the animal on the other side of the field lying near the fence. It reared up on its hind legs like a man. Rismiller says it is yellowish-brown in color, has no hair, small eyes and face, arms about fourteen inches long, legs somewhat longer, the hands and feet resembling those of a human being, and has two horns on the top of the head. The young men made a raid on the monster, when they say it darted toward the forest and was soon lost in the foliage. A Mr. Heckman, also residing near there, is reported to have seen the beast, and he is inclined to believe that it is a large-sized ape, that may have escaped from some traveling menagerie. Every cornfield is to be searched, together with the neighboring swamps, for the purpose of ascertaining what the young men have really seen. After the recent rains the farmers plainly saw very strange looking tracks in the sand on the road-side. They have also heard very unusual howls at night and the dogs of the neighborhood have been trying to hunt down the beast without success.[1]

◆

— A strange animal has lately been frightening some of the people around Nelson who have ventured near the woods north of that borough. The beast is described as black in color, with a long body and tail and very short legs, and of considerable size. Several persons say they have seen the animal, others have been followed by it, and many say that they have heard its horrible screeches. It makes a first class sensation.[2]

◆

The Huntingdon *Local News* of Saturday tells this snakey story: A peculiar snake or dragon was killed by Richard Roper, foreman of the Star ore mine near Shade Gap, this county, a few days ago. The reptile, we are credibly informed, was 7 feet 8 inches long, of a blueish color, and had two legs three inches long, and two feet one inch long, shaped like a human foot. It was impossible to capture the strange creature alive, as it showed fight, and Mr. Roper was obliged to kill it. We learn that the snake was photographed, so that doubting ones may have an opportunity of verifying the truth of the snake story.[3]

◆

THE SUSQUEHANNA ALLIGATOR.

A Story That Possibly Confirms That of the *Leader* of Several Years Ago.

The Carbondale *Leader* of Tuesday last has the following:

For several years, boatmen and others living along the Susquehanna between Susquehanna and Red Rock have been interested, not to say disturbed, by a creature in the water at the latter point. The strange marine animal always made its appearance at night, and an unearthly, weird noise, accompanied by splashing, have often awakened people from their slumbers. Along at the edge of the evening, a dark object has been seen slowly moving across the river, and boat after boat has been upset by it,

Last fall, a party returning from a harvest dance at John Dalton's were upset while crossing the stream, and two persons narrowly escaped being drowned. The majority of the party were of the opinion that the boat had collided with a log, but one or two keen-eyed ones solemnly affirmed that they had been pinched, while in the water, by some submarine monster. The animal did not confine its predatory excursions to the water but made occasional trips to the flats on either side, and many a farmer has suddenly missed sheep and calves. Several excursions have at different times been planned, and traps of all kinds have been set by the farmers to capture the strange monster, but the wary visitor managed to escape all the snares set for him.

A few evenings ago, while a dance was in progress at Michael Hagan's at Smoky Hollow, the festivities were interrupted by Bob Brown, who put his head inside the ball room and yelled: "For God's sake, boys, come down to the river quick! I've seen the whale, and he's taking a rest on the bank opposite the tannery."

Every man armed himself, and axes, log hooks, and picks seemed to be the favorite weapons. Rushing pell-mell to the river, the great animal was seen devouring a carcass of a sheep. As soon as he descried the posse, he dropped his supper, and slowly crawled into some bushes skirting the shore. The men thoroughly excited, hastily constructed a raft from some old flood trash and pushed out into the stream. They had not gone far, when the great jaws of the monster were set upon a board in the raft, but it was its death move, for in an instant every man on the raft attacked it. The monster made a terrible shriek, splashed the water violently, and finally with one loud expiring groan, sank beneath the surface, its blood coloring the waves. Securing a rope the body was hauled ashore, and by a lantern's dim rays it was found to be that of a monster alligator.

To say the captors were excited and delighted, would be drawing it mild. In an hour every inhabitant for miles around was present. Steelyards were secured, and the saurian was found to weigh 533 pounds. A physician from Hallstead, who is also a taxidermist, was sent out for and he soon arrived, along with a score of townspeople. He advised sending for Dr. Crozier, a noted taxidermist of Cornell University, who would probably purchase the carcass for a good round sum. It was therefore carefully housed and the people returned to their homes, glad that the terror of the Susquehanna was no more. Dr. Crozier arrived and was astonished, not only to find such a specimen of the saurian kind but that any had been found in the Susquehanna. He gave it as his opinion that years ago some residents hereabouts had been the owner of some pet alligator and that it at some time had escaped its confines, and since grown up along the marshes of the river. An old inhabitant believes that the late Isaac Griggs, formerly proprietor of the old National Hotel at Great Bend, once owned a pet alligator, which was sent by a relative in Florida.

Dr. Crozier paid the captors $50 and left for Ithica, taking with him the carcass.[4]

───────◆───────

Monongahela River's Awful Monster Twenty Feet Long.

While rowing on the upper Monongahela river near McClane's Landing, Earl Cain and William Bentley, of Masontown, were almost thrown out by some monster that struck the stern of their boat. The unknown animal came at them with eyes shining like balls of fir and mouth wide open, while its tail lashed the water into foam. Cain struck the animal a blow between the eyes which stunned it for a moment, when the monster upset the boat and broke it into a multitude of pieces, while the boys swam for the shore. It started after them, after the boat was demolished, and was seen by dozens of persons, who were summoned by the two adventurers.

This strange monster is said to have been seen a number of times in the past ten years, about this time of the year. Benjamin Provins, the ferryman, had an encounter with it five years ago and describes it as having a head like a horse, covered all over the body with scales, and is about 15 to 20 feet long.

Wharfmaster Wilson says he saw this serpent going up the river early in the spring, but thought he wouldn't say anything about it, for fear the government would not care to buy the Monongahela if it had a snake like that in it.[5]

---◆---

FISH WALKS LIKE A MAN.

Strange Animal Alarms Pennsylvania Residents Along Susquehanna.

York City, Pa., Oct. 22 — People residing along the river midway between Cly and Goldsboro are mystified and some alarmed over the sight of a strange creature that has its abode in the Susquehanna. Thus far but two men and their wives have seen the "thing." As it was seen in broad daylight more credence is given to the story than would be if it had it been seen at night, when people are more prone to see "things." The strange creature, whether fish or animal, is described as being as large as a man.

When seen it came up out of the water erect like a man walking and is described as looking like a man without arms.

Those persons who have seen it declare that they are not the victims of an optical illusion.[6]

---◆---

WATER SNAKE WITH WINGS

Reptile in Allegheny River Rivals Famed Sea Serpent.

Warren, Pa., Sept. 8. — Persons at Grunderville, three miles below this town, are excited over the appearance in the Allegheny river of a strange water monster in the form of a serpent with wings.

Miss Rachel Talbot, daughter of W. A. Talbot, who has a summer villa opposite Grunderville, was first to see the creature swimming up the middle of the river, the head protruding several feet above the surface. She called to "Hank" Jackson, ferryman for the Warren Lumber company, who ran for his rifle and opened fire.

Immediately the reptile reared its head at least 10 feet in the air, Jackson says, and charged for the shore, its eyes as big as saucers, fixed on him.

Jackson steadied himself and, taking careful aim, the bullet hit one of the wings, disabling it.

Jackson says the snake

finally flew as high as the ferry cable, which hangs 20 feet above the water, and then vanished.[7]

———————◆———————

FARMERS SEE A STRANGE ANIMAL

Loaded Guns Ready For Beast That Leaves Footprint Like Human Hand.

The residents of Bear Gap, Paxinos, Reed station and in the vicinity of Snydertown are greatly excited over the appearance of a large freak animal which has been making visits to the above places several nights each week for the past two weeks.

The animal was first seen near Bear Gap by Jacob Leisenring, a timber dealer. Mr. Leisenring was driving his automobile along the Brush Valley road toward Bear Gap, when he was surprised to see a large animal along the side of the road some distance ahead. The electric headlights on his automobile temporarily blinded the beast, but as it discovered the approach of the car it slunk into the bushes. Later, the tracks were found in the dust and resembled the imprint of a man's hand, although much smaller and apparently turned backward. Mr. Leisenring described the beast as having been about thirty inches in height about three feet long and seemed to be fur-covered, although he was unable to discern the color.

Last week, Irvin Startzel, of Shamokin, was driving an automobile along the creek road near Reed station, when a large animal, similar in size to the one seen by Mr. Leisenring, leaped across the road and disappeared on the mountain. The occupants of the car all declare that the animal was striped and leaped somewhat like the movements of an ape or monkey. They, too, saw the tracks in the dust and describe them similarly to those described by Mr. Leisengring.

Farmers in the vicinity of Paxinos and Elysburg have caught a glimpse of the animal and have heard a peculiar cry at night. No one has been able to get sufficiently close to ascertain exactly the characteristics of the beast. Guns and revolvers have been loaded and everyone in the rural districts is anxious to get a shot at the freak animal. However, no one has reported any damage done and many are anxious to capture the beast in traps which have been set in several places.[8]

———————◆———————

In the course of turning up the articles for the main portion of this book, I came across some additional stories of strange, non-bigfoot creatures in Pennsylvania. Those who have interest in bigfoot may find these stories entertaining and/or informative as well.

[1] *The Indiana Progress* (Indiana, PA) October 16, 1879.

[2] *The Wellsboro Gazette* (Wellsboro, PA) December 4, 1883.

[3] *The Shippensburg Chronicle* (Shippensburg, PA) July 28, 1887.

[4] *The Union Leader* (Wilkes-Barre, PA) July 26, 1889.

[5] *The Daily Republican* (Monongahela, PA) August 23, 1897.

[6] *The Wilkes-Barre Record* (Wilkes-Barre, PA) October 23, 1905.

[7] *Greenville Evening Record* (Greenville, PA) September 8, 1906.

[8] *The Danville Morning News* (Danville, PA) September 15, 1913.

APPENDIX IV

ALTERNATE NAMES FOR BIGFOOT IN PENNSYLVANIA

In the past, and even up through today, bigfoot haven't always been "bigfoot". Some locales have their own names for the creatures which were in use either before the terms bigfoot, sasquatch, et al. became commonplace or because bigfoot was, in their minds, the creature from the Pacific Northwest and therefore not the same beast prowling through Pennsylvania.

It may be a help to researchers to know these localized terms. I talked to one witness who told me that we do not have bigfoot in Pennsylvania. He then proceeded to tell me a story about big, hairy, upright walking creatures that lived on the mountains above the town where he lived. He called these creatures "hoedads" - a name he had learned as a child. "Hoedads" by his description, are the same thing as bigfoot, but for one reason or another this man knew them by the local term and considered them to be different creatures. Sometimes it is a matter of knowing what to ask.

The following is an incomplete list of alternate names for bigfoot creatures used in Pennsylvania. These names come from various places in Pennsylvania - some are from folklore or local legends, some are from the First Nations people, and others appear in articles in this volume.

Albatwitch / Albatwitcher / Elbatwitch*

Ape-Man

Cookie Monster

Ge no sqwa

Gettysburg Gorilla

Gorilla-Man

Gum Devil

Hairy-Man

The Hidebehind

Hoedad

Madman of the Woods

Man-Ape

Mesingw

Mirygdy

The Monster of the Mountains

Mowglis

Old Man of the Forest / Old Man of the Woods

Stone Giants

Stone Coats

Tree Walkers

The Whistling Wild Boy of the Woods*

Wild-Man / Wild-Man of the Woods

Windigo

Wooden-Face

Wookalar

Woolybooger / Woolybugger

*These names seem to refer to albatwitch or "little people".

INDEX OF PLACE NAMES

A

Abbottstown 23
Abingdon (MD) 154-155
Accomac 107-108
Adams County 142-143, 144, 148
Adamstown 11
Aleona 70
Allegheny 40, 62, 73
Allegheny Mountains 17, 26, 66
Allegheny River 173
Allentown 28
Altoona 23, 62, 128, 165
Amberson Valley 137
Armstrong County 22
Austinburgh 25
Avalon Borough 75, 77
Avon Borough 77
Avondale 112

B

Baldwin Township 122
Bear Creek 79
Bear Gap 174
Beaver Meadow 94
Bedford County 140
Bedminster 164
Ben Avon 76-77, 89
Bennington 16
Berks County 10, 12, 22, 28-29, 158, 169
Bethel Camp Ground 69
Big Run 32-33
Biglerville 146-147
Bird's Eye Pond 63
Blair County 7, 16, 131, 136

Bloomfield 161
Blue Knob 66
Blue Mountain 10
Blue Ridge 144
Boliver 45-46
Bottstown 9
Bradshaw (MD) 154
Bridgeville 25, 69
Bridgewater 2
Brownsville 46
Brush Mountain 23
Brush Run 130

C

Cambria County 139
Campbell's Mills 29
Canoe Creek 128-129, 131
Carbon County 9
Carlisle 9
Carnegie 113
Carre Hill 70
Cashtown 138
Chester 78-79, 80, 82-83, 112
Chester County 10, 53, 81
Chestnut Hill 74
Chestnut Hills 53
Chestnut Ridge 45
Chimney Rocks 129-130
Clarion County 16, 49
Claysburg 133, 141
Clayville 33
Clearfield County 7
Clifton Heights 82-83
Clinton County 42, 71
Cly 173
Coal Valley 49
Coaldale 64

Colebrook 65
College Hill 63
Columbia 94-95
Columbia County 93
Conewago Hills 65
Connellsville 75
Corry 70
Cove 105
Coventryville 53
Cross Keys 130
Crystal Lake 51
Cumberland 59
Cumberland County 142-143, 157
Cumberland (MD) 140
Curwensville 30

D

Danville 108-109, 111
Darby 79, 82-84, 86
Delano Mountain 166
Delaware County 79-80, 82-84, 86-87, 112
Doerr Terrace 118
Dry Gap 134
Dry Run 122
Duncannon 105
Duncansville 130
Dundaff 51
Dunmore 61, 62, 65, 66

E

Eaglesmere 92
East Berlin 90
East Rochester 103
Easton 3
Ebervale Mountain 166
Edenburg 49
Edenville 138
Edgewood (MD) 154-155
Eldorado 130

Elk Creek 47
Elk Mountain 50, 51
Elkdale 51
Elmsworth Borough 77
Elysburg 174
Emaus 164
Erie 39
Erie County 70

F

Fairfield 148
Fairmont 72
Fairview 46
Fallbrook Mountain 46
Farmington 88
Florence 45
Flourtown 29
Forks 25
Fort Louden 147
Franklin County 138, 143, 147-148
Franklintown 142
Freeland 166
Frog Hollow 72
Frugality 62
Fulton 65
Fulton County 65

G

Galeton 41-43, 70
Gardners 147
Gaysport Borough 135
Gaysport Reservoir 134
Gebhartsville 7
Georgetown 77, 79
Germantown 74
Gettysburg 141-142, 146-147
Gilbertsville 87
Ginger Hill 122
Girard Bank 4
Girardville 72

Glenshaw 162-163
Goldsboro 173
Grantville Gap 132
Great Bend 172
Greencastle 41
Greensburg 45
Greenville 67
Grunderville 173

H

Hallstead 44, 172
Hamburg 10, 28
Hammersly Fork 42
Hancock 44
Hanover 10
Harmonsburg 68
Harrisburg 8, 138
Harveys Lake 110
Havre De Grace (MD) 155
Haydock Mountain 89
Hays 122
Hays Borough 74, 120
Hazleton 106
Henderson Township 32
Hollidaysburg 66, 129, 134-135
Homestead Park 121
Horntown 81
Hughesville 17
Hummelstown 161
Hunter's Creek 109
Hunter's Station 69, 160
Hyde Park 40
Hyner 71

I

Idaville 142, 144
Indiana County 52
Intercourse 38
Ithica (NY) 172

J

Jackson 26
Jamison City 93
Johnstown 66
Jonestown 165
Joppa (MD) 154
Juniata County 137
Juniata River 132

K

Kellyville 83
Kennett Square 60
Kent's Mills 83
Kettle Creek 70-71
Kilbuck Township 76
Kinderhook 107
Kladder 135

L

Lake Erie 157
Lake Scranton 66
Lamokin Run 81
Lancaster 7, 94
Lancaster County 10, 27, 107
Laporte 47, 92
Laurel Run 77, 79
Lebanon 160
Lebanon County 158
Lehigh Mountain 28, 164
Leidy 42
Leiperville 112
Lemon Hill 165
Lewistown 108, 123-127, 131, 133
Lewistown Narrows 123, 126-127, 131, 133
Ligonier 46, 75
Ligonier Valley 25
Little Loyaisock 47

Lofty Mountain 165
Loop Station 129
Lower Mahanoy Valley 69
Lowrys Run 75
Luzerne Borough 26

M
Macedonia Gap 161
Madison Township 16
Magnolia (MD) 154
Mahaffy 30, 32-33
Maitland 145
Manayunk 44
Marietta 107
Marsh Creek 71
Marysville 105-106
Masontown 172
Mausdale 109
Mcconnellsburg 65
Mcclane's Landing 172
Mckeesport 49
McVeytown 108
Media 79
Media Park 81
Meiser 123, 125, 131
Meiserville 127
Middleburg 40, 123, 132, 134
Mifflin County 126, 131
Mifflin Township 60, 118-122
Middle Spring 137, 138
Middleburg 41
Millerstown 132
Monongahela River 172-173
Monterey 144-145
Moosic 108
Morgantown 10, 22
Morrisdale 140
Morton 78, 79
Mount Joy 73
Mount Manotome 44
Mount Penn 64-65, 68

Mount Rock 141
Mountainville 164
Mountville 95
Muhlenberg Township 169
Muncy Valley 92

N
Nanticoke 90
Nanticoke Mountain 90
Nay Aug Park 62
Nelson 170
Nero 45
Nescopeck 148
New Bedford 40
New Bergen 71
New California 22
New Holland 38
New Homestead 118-120, 122
New York City (NY) 33
Newburg 137-138
Newcomertown 136-138
Newfield 18
Newmanstown 158-160
Newport 165-166
Nicktown 32
Norristown 45
North Creek 43

O
Oak Hill 82
O'Hara Township 60
Oliver Township 109
Orrstown 138

P
Parkesburg 11
Patton 139
Paxinos 174
Pen Mar 59, 144-145
Penn Township 89

Pennsburg 87
Perkiomen 87
Perry County 8, 105
Peter's Mountain 51, 59
Petrolia 25
Philadelphia 79, 84, 86, 133
Pike County 70
Pittsburgh 76, 122, 161-162, 164, 166
Pittson 87
Porter's Point 105
Potter County 41-43
Pottstown 49, 53
Providence 63
Punxsutawny 33
Putnamville 105

Q
Quakertown 89
Quittapahilla Creek 104

R
Randolph Township 68
Reading 28, 68
Red Rock 171
Reed Station 174
Reidmore 140
Reymeyer's Valley 164
Richards Wood 49
Richill Township 113
Ridley Creek 112
Ridley Township 112
Ringtown 24, 72
Rochester 103
Rockville 8
Roselawn 129-130
Rouzerville 143-145
Roxbury 137
Ruchsville 9
Ruscombmanor Township 169
Russell 105

Rutherford 31
Ryerson Station 113

S
Saeger's Woods 10
Salisbury 164-165
Sam City 18
Saratoga 49
Schaefferstown 158-159
Scranton 40, 62, 65-66
Selinsgrove 128
Seven Mountains 146
Seven Valleys 167
Shade Gap 170
Shade Mountain 161
Shamokin 69, 174
Sharon Hill 83-84
Shenandoah 24
Shippensburg 137-138, 141
Silver Lake Township 2
Slam Bang 18
Smoky Hollow 44, 171
Snyder County 123, 125-128, 131, 139
Snydertown 174
Somerset County 7
South Mountain 26, 28, 39
Sprigles Valley 49
Springfield 78, 80
Springfield Township 78-81, 86
Spruce Run 89
St. Clair 24
Stockton 166
Strawbridge 93
Stroudsburg 108
Sullivan County 92-93
Sunbury 134
Susquehanna 44, 171
Susquehanna County 50
Susquehanna River 171-173
Swatara 165

Swatara Creek 104, 161
Swatara Gap 12

T

Tamaqua 64, 72
Taylorstown 75
Tillberry's Knob 91
Tioga County 71
Tionesta 160
Topton Station 169
Turkey Hill 44
Twolick Hills 52, 112

U

Undercliff 162-164
Upland 83
Upper Bern Township 10

V

Valley Township 22
Verona 88-89

W

Wallaceton 139
Warren 173
Washington County 25

Washington 93
Waynesboro 143
Waynesburg 113, 118
Weatherly 94
Wellsboro 43
Welsh Mountain 10, 22, 27-28
West Branch Valley 42
West End 137
West Grove 39
West Mead Township 68
West Mountain 40
Westfield 94
Whiskey Run 78
Wilkes-Barre 77, 85, 110
Williamsburg 135-136
Williamsport 103, 123-125, 127, 129
Wilna (MD) 154
Wilson's Woods 49
Wissahickon Creek 74
Womelsdorf 26-28, 39-40, 158

Y

Yatesville Borough 87
York 173
York County 46, 142
York Springs 142, 147

ABOUT THE AUTHOR

Timothy Renner is an illustrator, author, paranormal investigator, and folk musician living in York County, Pennsylvania. His illustrations have appeared in the pages of various books, magazines, fanzines and comics as well as on many record and CD covers. Since 1995, Timothy has been making music both solo and with his band, Stone Breath. Stone Breath has released over a dozen albums. Timothy's first book, *Beyond the Seventh Gate* was published in 2016. Timothy is the co-host of *Strange Familiars*, a podcast concerning the paranormal, weird history, folklore and the occult. He makes regular appearances on the paranormal radio show, *Where Did the Road Go?*, and has appeared as a guest on many other podcasts and radio programs, including *Coast to Coast AM*.

contact Timothy via email: TimeMothEye@gmail.com

photo by: A.E. Hoskin

Made in the USA
Columbia, SC
09 June 2020